Ephesians

The Church, the Bride of Christ

First published 2011

ISBN No: 978-1-905975-32-7

Published by Biblical Frameworks

Reg. Office: 23 Coe Lane, Tarleton, Preston. PR4 6HH

Cover design, typesetting and production management by
Verité CM Ltd, Worthing, West Sussex UK +44 (0) 1903 241975

Illustrations by Richard Thomas

Printed in England

Biblical Frameworks is registered in England No: 5712581
Charity No: 1116805.

Contents

1. Introductory thoughts from Paul Blackham

The longest chapter in the Bible is all about... the Bible! Psalm 119 is all about the wonder of the Word of God. Verse 103 shows us the heart of someone who really loved the Bible. He cries out to the LORD God:

Psalm 119:103 – "How sweet are your words to my taste, sweeter than honey to my mouth!"

Whether you are reading the Bible alone or in some kind of group with others, expect to be thrilled by the words of the Living God. This is not like reading any other book. When we read and study the Bible the ultimate Author can be present with you, showing you His words and applying them to you.

Thousands of small groups are starting up all over the world – but what is it that is going to sustain them? It has to be the Bible.

So often, people don't quite know what to do with these small groups. Meeting together, sharing testimonies and experiences or sharing the odd verse is ultimately too sparse a diet to sustain people's spiritual needs in the long run, and really help them to grow.

What is needed is confidence in the Bible, and the ability to go to a *book* of the Bible rather than just an isolated verse. Each book of the Bible was written with a purpose, and it is only as we digest it as a book that we understand the real message, purpose, direction, storyline and characters.

It's a lot easier than people often think. You might think, "Oh, I can't manage a whole book of the Bible", but what we're trying to do in Book by Book is to break it down and show that it's easy.

The Bible was written not for specialists, not for academics – it was written for the regular believers, down the ages.

The world is in desperate need for answers. How can the world live at peace? How can we live together with justice and truth and compassion? There are so many religions and so much division and bloodshed: what is the real and living way that takes us to the Living God who can give us all a new beginning?

The Bible is the answer of the Living God to all our questions.

Our desire is that many Christians would experience the joy and confidence in the Scriptures that is found throughout Psalm 119 – "How sweet are your words to my taste, sweeter than honey to my mouth!"

II. All about Book by Book

A. WHAT IS BOOK BY BOOK?

Book by Book is a Bible study resource with accompanying DVD. It has been designed principally for use in small groups, but can also be used for personal study or larger group situations.

B. THE STRUCTURE OF BOOK BY BOOK

The Study Guide

- A Key Truth to focus on the most important truth in that section of the Bible Book.
- A Mind-Map diagram giving an overview of the study.
- An explanation of the Bible text, divided under suitable headings.
- Further Questions to stimulate deeper thought and discussion.
- A week of suggested daily Bible readings to fill out and explore the themes from the study.
- A Bible Study with detailed questions, designed to lead the individual or group deeper into the text.
- A Bible Study answers section at the back of the study guide, for extra help if need be.

The DVD

Key features provided on each DVD are as follows:

- There is a 15 minute discussion on the DVD linked to each section of the Study Guide Bible passage
- The on-screen host is Richard Bewes, with co-host Paul Blackham. A specially invited guest joins them in the Bible discussions.

C. SOME TIPS ON HOW TO USE BOOK BY BOOK

The beauty of Book by Book is that it offers not only great Biblical depth, but also flexibility of approach to study. Whether you are preparing to lead a small group, or study alone you will find many options open to you.

And it doesn't matter if you are a new Christian or more experienced at leading Bible studies, Book by Book can be adapted to your situation. You don't need to be a specially trained leader.

Group study: preparing

- Select your study (preferably in the order of the book!)
- Watch the DVD programmes
- Read the commentary
- Use the suggested Bible Questions...

  ...or formulate your own questions (the Mind Maps and Key Truths are a great guide for question structure).

Group study: suggested session structure

We recommend you set aside about an hour for each study:

- 5 minutes – read the relevant section of the Bible
- 15 minutes – Watch the DVD programme
- 30 minutes – work through the Bible Questions (either your own or the ones in the guide), allowing time for discussion
- 10 minutes – If the study got the group thinking about wider issues of life today, then consider the Further Questions to stimulate a broader discussion
- Taking it further – Suggest that group members look at some of the Daily Readings to follow up on the theme of the study

Given the volume of material you may even choose to take two weeks per study – using the DVD to generate discussion for one week and the Bible Questions for the next.

Individual study

There is no set way to conduct personal study – here are some ideas:

- Select your study (preferably in the order of the book!)
- Read the Bible passage and related commentary.
- Try looking at the Mind-Map diagrams and seeing how the book has a structure.
- Take a look at the Key Truths and decide if they are the same conclusions you had reached when you read the book.
- Perhaps focus on the week of daily Bible reading to help you to explore the rest of the Bible's teaching on the themes of each section of study.
- Work through the Bible Questions. Don't worry if you get stuck, there is an 'answers' section at the back of the guide!

III. An introduction to Ephesians

The book of Ephesians is the most thorough and wide-ranging account of what it means to be the Church, in the New Testament.

The story of the Bible is not the story of how isolated individuals may be saved. This story is a huge, cosmic story involving the heavens and the earth. It is the story of how the Church is saved. The creation and redemption of the whole universe is not to provide a place for mere individuals to wander around, but to establish the glorious home of the Living God with His united family forevermore.

Right now in our local Church families we may experience something of that glorious kingdom of the Living God on earth. In our local Church, as we work together to live the way of Jesus, as we die to ourselves in serving each other, as we answer the needs of the local Church family, as we learn to put the needs of our brothers and sisters ahead of our own, so we begin to find the very centre of the destiny of the universe, the eternal plans of the Living God.

The Ephesian Christians lived in the shadow of the massive temple to Artemis, as we read in Acts 19. That 'wonder of the ancient world' must have dominated not only the skyline but also the thinking of the city. The followers of Jesus must have been constantly bombarded with ideas and assumptions from their old non-Christian life. If they listened to those ideas and began to think like that again, they would slip into a terrible pit of despair, disillusionment, insensitivity and depression, even feeling as if they were cut off from God again. The Church was the oasis of sanity in that pagan chaos and confusion, the place where the truth of Jesus was lived and taught. The Church was the place where they could encourage one another in the truth that they learned in Jesus, the truth that came to them from the Living God Himself.

We must never over-spiritualize the Church. Liz and I have several friends who never go to Church at all yet still claim to be in some sense 'Christians'. They just shrug their shoulders and say, "well, I am a member of the *invisible* Church, the spiritual Church." They say that all the churches around them are not pure enough, not Biblical enough, not relevant, not loving enough, too traditional, too 'modern', not welcoming

enough, not how they want a Church to be etc. I heard about one man who said that he couldn't find even one Church in a large city that was 'sound' enough for him.

The apostle Paul could easily have said such things about the churches in Galatia or in Corinth. But he didn't. He got involved to love them and serve them. There are no solitary Christians in the New Testament. Every Christian is a member of a local Church. The local Church is the Body of Christ. If I refuse to join a local Church then there is something deeply wrong with my relationship to Jesus.

I cannot claim to follow Jesus if I reject His Body.

The generous and self-sacrificial life of the local Church is like a shining beacon in the darkness, the warm lights of home on a dark and stormy night. When we live together as Jesus commanded us, as the apostle Paul sets out in this letter to the Ephesians, then the world can see the truth and power of the gospel of Jesus. Even the most sinister spiritual powers of darkness are defeated when the good news of Jesus is really believed in the local Church.

Acts chapter 19 tells us all we need to know about the city of Ephesus. When Paul arrived he found believers who had heard the teaching of John the Baptist and were still waiting for the Messiah to come (Acts 19:1-7), still waiting for the Lamb of God who would take away the sins of the world – John 1:29. These Gentile[1] followers of John the Baptist did not know that Jesus had now accomplished everything that the prophets had foretold, that He had already been sacrificed as the Lamb of God and opened up the life of Israel to the whole world, regardless of nationality, religious background or geography. They did not realize yet that through Jesus' death, resurrection and ascension they, even as Gentiles, could experience the Holy Spirit just as the believing Jews had always done.

1 "Gentile" simply means "non-Jewish". The Jews were a distinct mixed group formed of descendents of Abraham as well as other people who had given up their own nationality to join the Jewish nation (see Exodus 12:38 for a classic example of other nations joining Israel). All the other people of the world were called 'the Gentiles' so some translations of the Bible simply use the word 'foreigners' to capture this meaning.

The Church of the Living God had been contained in regional or national limits built by the Law of Moses, yet those limits had been broken down and the Church was 'going global', spreading out to every nation, drawing both Jews and Gentiles in as one people, one fellowship, one undivided family.

In Acts 19 we see how Paul quite deliberately moved his Bible study meetings from the Jewish synagogue to the lecture hall of Tyrannus so that all the Jews and the Gentiles could hear the word of the LORD together (Acts 19:8-12).

Ephesus was a city full of spiritual darkness and occult power. The unbelieving Jewish 'ghostbusters' were unable to control these demonic powers, yet the Name of Jesus was demonstrated to have final authority even over these powerful spiritual forces. In the light of this, the Gentiles in Ephesus turned away from their occult beliefs and practices (Acts 19:13-20).

The presence of the Church of Jesus in Ephesus caused a profound social revolution. The worship of the pagan goddess Artemis was a very profitable enterprise for Ephesus. She was held to be the woman clothed in divine majesty for the whole world (Acts 19:27). The followers of Jesus had avoided any direct criticism of this pagan worship (Acts 19:37), yet they were living in such a different way that it created a genuine crisis for the city.

If pagan Ephesus thought that it was all about a great cosmic woman, Paul wrote this letter all about the real "cosmic woman", the Bride of Jesus, the Church.

Paul's letter to the Ephesians will take us down into the heart of our lives together in the local Church. Do we provoke crises or revolutions in our own cities because of the way we live together? Why is it so important to be part of a local Church? How is the local Church the answer to the social problems of the world? Why is it the proper context for our marriages to work, for our children to grow up, for our careers to find their true ambition?

Why is the Church the very centre of the universe?

Stand! Therefore

Study 1 The Church is at the centre of the universe Ephesians 1:1-23

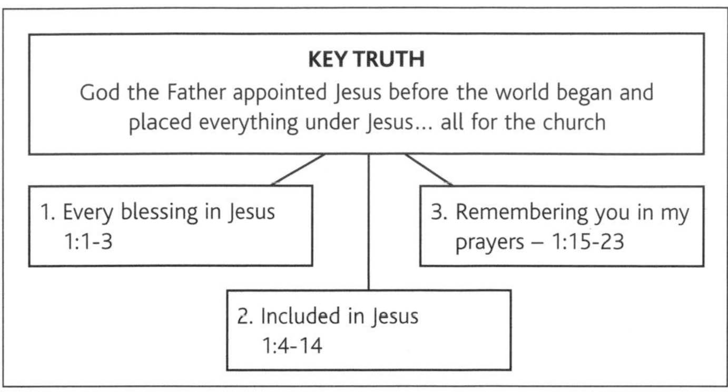

1. Every blessing in Jesus – 1:1-3

There is one big truth about the Church we all can grasp. The Church is at the centre of the universe. The Church was in the mind of God before He created the universe.

Paul was appointed by Jesus the Messiah Himself and this was intended by the Living God – verse 1. In the shadow of the mighty temple to Artemis at Ephesus, there was a local Church: a local fellowship of Jesus-followers. They may have felt small and insignificant yet from the highest heaven God the Father and the LORD Jesus Christ sent them special friendship and peace – verse 2.

From one perspective our local Church may seem to be completely overshadowed by all the other forces in society, but from the perspective of the throne room of the universe, the local Church is at the very centre, the most important group in any society. Ephesians chapter 1 teaches us that in one sense the Church as the Body of Christ is the reason that there is a universe!

One of the most vocal opponents of Christianity argues that as we look out at the inconceivable vastness of the universe, we should come to an awareness of how pitifully small and irrelevant we are. Yet, Paul says the opposite. Before the world began the Eternal Father chose a bride for His Eternal Son: a bride that would share His very life; a bride that would be accepted and loved by the Father just as the Father accepts and loves His Eternal Son. When we look out at the sheer size of the universe, we should be filled with worship, awe and wonder that the Eternal Father, Son and Holy Spirit have made us so incredibly significant.

As we consider the grandeur of the universe, we are to marvel, with David in Psalm 8, that through Jesus, the Creator's mind is full of care for us. The Father's infinite love for the Son of Man overflows down onto His Body, His Church, His Bride.

Jesus Christ is the treasure chest containing every blessing for the Church – verse 3.

2. Included in Jesus – 1:4-14

Notice throughout this first chapter how Paul puts Jesus at the very centre of the heavens and the earth and then he explains how the Church exists right inside Jesus Himself. Everything about the Church is 'in Jesus'. A fish lives in water and its food, oxygen, movement, life and society is all *in water*. A fish out of water has nothing at all, but a fish in water has everything that it needs.

My eye is in Paul Blackham! Because my eye is in me, then it shares my life. It goes where I go. It has all the privileges that I have, all the life experiences and blessings that I have. When I unlock my front door and go into my private office, my eye gets to come too! When I get to meet interesting people, my eye gets to see them too! In me, my eye has everything that I have.

These are ways of understanding this profound teaching about the true nature of the Church. Jesus shares His entire life and privileges with His Church. Think of a human body where He is the head and the Church is the body; think of a vine where He is the main stem and the Church is all the branches drawing life from the stem; think of bricks all built on a big solid foundation stone. This Biblical language is drawing us deeper and deeper into this glorious and mysterious truth: the life of the Eternal Son is holistically and completely shared with the Church.

The Father first gives every possible blessing to Jesus, and then unites the Church to Jesus. Paul didn't invent this marvellous fact: Jesus Himself taught all this in John 17. Just as the Father loved Jesus before the world began, so He loves the Church – John 17:23. Just as Jesus is united to the Father, so the Church also enjoys this incredible union – John 17:20-21. Just as Jesus enjoyed a divine and eternal glory with the Father before the world began, so the Church also shares in this wondrous glory – John 17:22. The words of the apostle Paul would seem impossible unless Jesus Himself taught all this.

We can easily see how Jesus is the One He loves, the One who is holy and blameless in His sight, His own eternal Son. It is easy to see how the Father could make an eternal choice for such a One! Yet, the fact that this love and choice for the holy and blameless Jesus is also extended to the whole Church is 'glorious grace'. Before any of us had ever done anything at all, before we even existed, the Father purposed a wife for His Son, a Church that would be one flesh with His Son, sharing all the blessings, love and privilege that He had for His Eternal Son.

For most of the history of the world any long journey was a very risky venture. There was no guarantee that travellers would arrive at their destination. However, the Gracious and Loving Father planned the destiny, the life and eternal home of the Church before the world began.[2] Nothing was left to chance. He set the destination of the Church to be living the life of Jesus, adopted into God's family, in an everlasting creation.

Why would the Father make such a difficult plan? Guaranteeing such a glorious destiny for the Church is surely an impossible task, especially when we consider the building materials for the Church. As we evil, selfish and wretched people trust in Jesus, so we are included in Him (verse 13)! The Father guarantees such a glorious destiny for the Church because He is filled with love and it pleases Him to give such wonderful blessings to those who don't deserve anything – verses 4-6. Yes, we will eternally praise Him for the loving friendship that He has freely given to us.

2 The eternal family home of the Son and His Wife was planned from the very beginning. The Church's final appearance and presence at the marriage feast of the Lamb has been a guiding principle for the whole universe since it began.

In verses 7-8 Paul reminds us how the Father prepared for even the worst of us. The Eternal Beloved Son gave His own blood to redeem us, to forgive our sins, to give us the richest, most loving fellowship with the Living God.

In the modern world we too easily translate the language of blood into relational and psychological words. When we look back through the Scriptures (and even into the ancient human religions of the world), we see how deeply valuable blood is. Peace with God is bought with blood. Blood is the very life of a creature, taking energy to the whole body and taking away all that needs to be purified from the body. From the very beginning of the world, blood is needed to purify from uncleanness, to pay the price of sin. Our sin has consequences far beyond what our physical eyes may see. In a profound and mysterious way, the cost of our sin is paid in blood: not in good deeds or religion. The blood of animals was never sufficiently precious to cover this cost, never enough to purify us, yet from the beginning the promise of the Divine Lamb's blood sustained the ancient Church. The rivers of blood flowing through the ancient Hebrew Scriptures were all flowing towards the blood of Jesus: the blood of God (Acts 20:28; see also Hebrews 9:12; 13:12). Here is blood that can atone and cleanse from every sin and uncleanness. Here is blood that is more precious than we can ever imagine. Here is blood that can be sprinkled on us to show that judgment has already fallen. Here is blood that can soothe even the righteous anger of the Living God.

The fact that the Living God will do whatever it takes to redeem the Church to the destiny He has purposed will always fill us with awe and wonder and worship. His wisdom and understanding is so great (verse 8) that He found a way to soothe His own heart about our vile sin; a way to not only display His hatred of our evil but also to forgive us freely; a way to not merely tolerate us but lavish His love on us.

Furthermore, we might assume that we could never know the deepest secrets of the Infinite Living God. How could we ever find out let alone understand what the Eternal Trinity is doing? Yet, in verses 9 and 10, Paul tells us that it pleases the Father to reveal all His secrets to the Church! He doesn't hide from us His purposes, but brings us in on all that He is doing. We know where history has come from and where it is heading.

Fate was the dominant word of the ancient Greek and Roman gods. Human beings are puppets of Fate, unable to escape what has been decided for them. In the modern world a new fatalism threatens. The modern mythmakers tell us stories in which we are the meaningless products of random, impersonal forces; that our actions are all determined by mechanical biology/neurology; that brute determinism lies behind all our pretence of purpose so that nothing we ever do really matters; that good and evil are nothing more than ever-changing social constructions; that finally the earth itself will whimper out in cosmic decay.

The Father holds nothing back, openly telling us that Jesus is the key to everything. The heavens and the earth, the galaxies and the angels, the skies and the earth, the plants and animals, history and humanity, all find their function, purpose and destiny in Jesus. More than any cosmologist, the Church understands how the universe itself is heading to a fulfilment when everything is brought together under Jesus Christ. [3]

Can we imagine how these words must have sounded to that Ephesian Church gathering in the shadow of the temple of Artemis? They might have felt as if the forces that were controlling the world had nothing to do with the Way of Jesus: the Roman Empire; the Greek and Roman gods; the religious economy of Ephesus etc. Yet, in these opening verses of Paul's letter he has turned their view of the world upside down. The Church is at the very centre of the universe and the true history of the world is the history of the Church.[4]

We may not understand *why* everything happens as it does, but we can trust this glorious Father, who gives us His own Son, to bring the Church to that wonderful destiny that He purposed for us. Far from living meaningless lives, in Jesus we may find a purpose that actually brings glory to the Majestic God – verse 12.

3 This is obvious even now as we see the mind, the life, death and resurrection of Jesus reflected and expressed in the stars, the skies, the seasons, the oceans, the plants, the animals, even our own bodies. Can anybody witness the defeat of darkness by the light each morning without confessing that Jesus is LORD? Can any of us experience the daily descent into our death-like sleep and the resurrection of awakening without worshipping Jesus?

4 Notice how often Paul refers to the 'heavenly realms' – 1:3, 20; 2:6; 3:10; 4:8; 6:12. This letter is indirectly challenging all the religions of the world. If Jesus is the final and highest truth in the 'heavenly realms' then where do the other religions fit in?

Paul and the other Jewish believers were following Jesus before these Ephesians (verse 12), yet the Ephesians were also included in Jesus when they heard the message of Jesus and trusted Him (verse 13). Having believed in Jesus, we receive a special seal: a divine stamp that confirms and guarantees our life and future in Jesus.[5]

It is essential that the completed work of Jesus happens "outside of ourselves"; it is objective and we can trust in Him regardless of our own state of mind and heart. However, alongside that, we have the subjective work of the Spirit, giving us a real and personal experience of the salvation that Jesus has achieved. Joy, peace, self-control, hope, love and fellowship are all gifts of the Spirit as He personally assures us of our relationship to the Father. As He builds the local Church and as we become involved in that fellowship so we experience His life and walk in step with Him.

We have been given God the Holy Spirit as a guarantee of all that has been promised to us. What has been promised to us? That even though we are sinful creatures, yet we receive the same inheritance as the Eternal Son. No matter what happens to the Church now, whether we are persecuted or even killed, yet the Father is so determined to grant us a future beyond our wildest imagination that He has placed the Holy Spirit within us as a deposit.

We put a deposit on something if we are determined to buy it later. Usually we just put a deposit of 10% of the purchase price. But the Living God has placed *Himself* as the deposit on our future. The Holy Spirit is, obviously, infinitely more valuable than the whole creation yet He stands as surety for our future. He is the engagement ring for our forthcoming marriage as we will see in chapter 5.

No matter how vulnerable or insignificant we may feel; no matter how intimidated we may be by the religions and ideologies of this world; no matter how dark the valley of the shadow of death may seem to us, yet

5 The Ephesians had a very specific experience of this. They believed the message of John the Baptist concerning the coming Messiah, the Lamb of God – Acts 19:4. However, it seems that they didn't know that Jesus had in fact arrived and done everything prophesied about Him. They did not know that the division between Jew and Gentile had been destroyed; therefore they did not know that they could experience the Holy Spirit just as the Jewish believers had done.

if we have trusted in Jesus and are following Him, the very life of the Trinity is placed on the line to guarantee that we arrive in that new creation future that will appear with Jesus.

The Church is 'God's possession' (verse 14). The Church is the place of safety, the foretaste of the future, the family of God, the Bride of Jesus, the hope of the world, the centre of the universe, the Body of Christ – and nothing in life should mean more to us than our love, service, fellowship and worship in our local Church as we follow Jesus together.

3. Remembering you in my prayers – 1:15-23

When Paul heard that the fellowship in Ephesus continued to trust Jesus and love one another (verse 15) he couldn't stop thanking the Father. There is nothing more exciting than the presence of a local Church in any city in the world. All other organizations and initiatives are trivial compared to this. We know that the Living God is at work when we see that He has gathered a local Church in the Name of Jesus. It may be hidden from the authorities and it may be suffering all kinds of persecution, rejected by the media and ridiculed by the elite, yet anything can happen when the Living God is working the deepest purposes of the universe in even the smallest local Church.

How do we pray for churches around the world? How do we pray for our own local Church? Sometimes our prayers are filled with 'shopping list' items: more money; bigger or better buildings; more people; more gifts and talents; more blessing for our plans; less trouble etc. Even though Paul knew about all the 'practical' needs of the Ephesian Church, yet his prayers for them were much deeper than a mere shopping list. In fact, his great prayer was that the Ephesian Church would have deeper *knowledge*.

He asked the Father for three aspects of knowledge for the Church: to know Him better (verse 17); to know the riches of our future hope (verse 18); and to know the great power at work in us (verse 19). It is good to meditate on why Paul asks for this knowledge rather than 'practical things'. If we know Him better then we will live more like Him and say no to the greed and evil desires of this passing age.

Verse 17 is one of the many great Trinitarian verses of the Bible. The glorious Father, the LORD Jesus and the Spirit of wisdom and revelation all work together so that we may know Him better. This reminds us of those words of Jesus from John 17:3 – "this is eternal life: that they may know you, the only true God, and Jesus Christ, whom you have sent." At the heart of everything is *knowing God*. He may give us all kinds of physical blessings now and forever, but none of them compare to knowing Him. All the money in the world, all the health and wealth, mean nothing unless we know Him. If we do know Him then we can be content in any circumstance, whether we have plenty or nothing, whether we are weak or strong, living or dying – Philippians 4:11-13. In fact in Philippians 3:8 Paul even declares "I consider everything a loss compared to the surpassing greatness of knowing Christ Jesus my Lord".

To live in a paradise forever, but to never know the LORD Jesus would in the end be a kind of Hell. We were created to know Him and when we try to satisfy that infinite desire with anything else we find our thirst constantly returning with renewed intensity. This is why Paul prays that the Church would be given the Holy Spirit of wisdom and revelation. The Church needs more than mere information: we need the Spirit Himself who will give us the living, vibrant reality that the Scriptures set before us.

In verse 18 Paul prays that the "eyes of your heart may be enlightened" so that the Church might know our great hope and the great power at work in us. What are "the eyes of your heart"? Jesus Himself referred back to the words of Isaiah chapter 6 when He explained how people need to see with their hearts – Matthew 13:13-15. Paul's fear was that the Ephesian Church might end up merely hearing all these glorious truths, but never truly grasping or understanding them. He prayed that the Spirit would come and be their Teacher within, making sure that as they studied the Scriptures together they really understood.

Paul prayed for this deep understanding in two specific areas: verse 18 – the hope of our rich inheritance; verse 19 – his incomparably great power at work in us.

Jesus was able to endure the Cross because He was so sure about the joy set before Him. If we are to follow Him, living a life of love and justice as

He did, then we too need to have a clear knowledge of the hope set before us. The heavens and the earth were created for Jesus (Colossians 1:16) and on the day that He inherits, He will renew everything (Matthew 19:28), preparing the universe to be the eternal home of righteousness (2 Peter 3:11-14). As heaven comes down to earth, so the new creation will be the family home of the Living God forever and ever. The marriage feast of the Lamb will be the first, glorious event as the history of the world begins its never-ending story.

The Bible is full of this resurrection hope and the world around us bears witness to this future in so many ways.[6] Our hope is for the "the riches of His glorious inheritance", so the money or possessions of this passing age could never hold onto us if we have got hold of this hope in our hearts, as Paul prayed. We can always tell whether a person really believes in the return of Jesus by the way that they live: how they give away their money; how they love their enemies; how they hunger and thirst for justice; how they care for the Church family.

All this might seem impossible, given our sinful natural instincts to be selfish, to store up our own security on earth, to be hard-hearted towards the needy, to hate or even ignore our enemies. This is why the second part of Paul's prayer is so vital. We need enlightened hearts to know our great hope, but also to know the incomparably great power that is at work in us – verse 19.

Verses 19-23 are Paul's description of the great power of the Living God at work within us. Philosophy talks about 'god' in such weird and abstract ways[7], yet here we learn where the sheer power of Almighty God is really exercised.

6 Jesus refers to the way that a seed dies and then produces a resurrection harvest (John 12:24). The terrors of the night are so easily dispelled by the bright hope of the morning. The eight-legged spider lives to destroy flies; the ant works hard for its future; the vegetarian ruminants live at peace; the water that rises to form the clouds falls again to bring such refreshing life and fertility. We might also notice how a caterpillar has such a glorious new body in its future.

7 Human philosophy works in 'power categories' that are all too human, speaking of 'power' in the ways that the flesh all too readily understands. What philosophy book argues that the greatest possible display of divine power is raising Jesus up to the highest place in the heavenly realms?

Think of the situation at the Cross on that Friday afternoon when Jesus died. The Immortal God died a cursed death, rejected by humanity and forsaken by His Father. The earth was covered in darkness, shaking at the horror of what had just happened. Yet, God's great power was at work even in that shameful death and from that deepest and darkest place the sheer omnipotence of the Living God would be shown as never before and never again. Jesus passed through death and created a new 'world' beyond. Others, like Lazarus, may have gone into death and then returned to mortal life, but Jesus went on through mortality into an immortal *physical* life that had never existed before. Through the Word a new creation appeared right out of this old one. One human-sized bit of the old creation was taken through into a new creation – and just as all the thread follows the needle, so the whole of this old creation will be pulled through into that new creation future when Jesus appears.

Furthermore, that new human, that Second Adam, walked out of the tomb and then was raised up to the highest heaven! (verse 20) When He died the curtain in the temple symbolically separating heaven and earth had been torn from top to bottom, so in His ascension He proves the reality of this. Jesus was exalted to the very highest place in heaven – having been down to the very lowest, place of sin and death. Every power, in fact, *every thing* is placed under the feet of Jesus. He rules over all things, not only now in this present age but also in that glorious new creation future to come. Just as everything exists because of Jesus and holds together because of Jesus and finds its purpose in Jesus, so He also fills everything with His resurrected and glorified presence.

Meditate carefully on verse 23, because it is one of the most mysterious verses in the whole Bible. The Church is the body of Jesus and He is the head. Yet, and here is the deepest mystery of all, the Church is described as the "fullness" of Jesus. In Colossians 1:19 we are told that God was pleased to have all His "fullness" dwell in Jesus.

Is Paul then saying that Jesus is pleased to have all His "fullness" in the Church, that everything that He is, without dilution or hesitation, flows into the Church? There are depths here that are beyond all we can think or imagine.

Study 1 Bible Questions

Ephesians 1:15-23

1. Verses 15-16. What two things about the Ephesians cause such thanksgiving in Paul's prayers? Is there any connection between these two things?
2. Verse 17. Although the whole Trinity is in this verse, what does Paul pray that the Spirit will do? How might this happen?
3. Verse 18. Paul prays for more knowledge for the Ephesians, yet this knowledge is not to be grasped by head but heart. Why does this particular knowledge need to be seen with the heart rather than the head?
4. Verse 19-20. What is the highest example of God's omnipotent power? Why was this such a supreme test for the power of the Living God? How is this same power at work in us?
5. Verse 21. Why do we need to know the extent of Christ's power and authority? What relevance did this have for the Ephesians and what does it mean for us?
6. Verses 22-23. What do we think of the Church? Does the Bible back up Paul's claim that the Church is at the very centre of the universe, the fullness of Christ Himself who rules everything for the Church? If we believed this, how would we treat our local Church? Do we need to change our priorities?

Study 1 Further Questions

1. When we think of the history of the universe, why is it so important to start from the right place? Is it sufficient to begin with a 'big bang'? Why does the Bible reach back to the 'time before time', the life of the Father, Son and Spirit before the universe began?
2. In most of the world and down through history it would be impossible to imagine being a Christian who does not go to Church. However, this is something that we find cropping up in parts of the Western world today. Why is this? What assumptions or experiences create such confusion? Could it ever be right to simply log onto an 'internet Church' each week for some 'Sunday worship and teaching'?
3. If the Ephesians were overshadowed by the temple of Artemis, then what are the great temples of our day that dominate our culture and thinking? How can our local Church help us to resist these forms of non-Christian thinking?

Study 1 Daily Readings

Day 1	Ephesians 1:1-14
Day 2	Ephesians 1:15-23
Day 3	Acts 19:1-22
Day 4	Acts 19:23-20:1
Day 5	John 17:1-5
Day 6	John 17:6-19
Day 7	John 17:20-26

The daily Bible readings are an opportunity to not only read through all of the material in the book under study, but also to read parts of the Bible that relate to the themes and issues that we have been considering. Wetry to make sure that we receive light from the whole Bible as we think through the key issues each week.

Study 2 The Church is God's workmanship
Ephesians 2:1-10

KEY TRUTH

The blessings, the fellowship and the diversity of the church are all the work of the Living God

1. By nature objects of wrath – 2:1-5

2. By grace you have been saved – 2:6-10

1. By nature objects of wrath – 2:1-5

After chapter one we may well feel a little light-headed, a bit overwhelmed by the importance of the Church. We may well begin to feel impressed that we are at the centre of all that God is doing with His creation. However, all the way through chapter 1 Paul emphasised that all the Church's blessings are *in Christ*.

When we consider the glorious privileges, status and destiny of the Church we all too often fall over into what is known as 'triumphalism': looking only at the future and heavenly glory without also seeing the present and earthly challenge. It is like looking only at the Resurrection of Jesus without seeing the Cross of Jesus.

To properly appreciate just how marvellous and majestic is the saving power of the Living God within us, we need to appreciate how bad we were, how far we had fallen from the presence of the Most High. We might have met Lazarus at the dinner party in John 12:1, but unless we also knew that Lazarus had been dead and rotting away for four days in John 11, then we would not appreciate the power of Jesus, the Resurrection and the Life.

If Ephesians chapter 1 puts the focus on Jesus and the Church's glory in Jesus, then now we learn what it was to be outside of Jesus. Paul gives us the sober diagnosis that we find throughout the whole Bible:

- Verse 1 – *we were dead in transgressions and sins.* As far as the life of God is concerned, as far as having a life that will keep on bubbling up forever and ever, we were dead, killed by our failures and rebellion. Not only do we constantly fall short of all we could be, but we also deliberately do what is evil.
- Verse 2 – *we followed the ways of the world.* We were caught up in the stream, carried along with everybody else, following along with the patterns and assumptions that that allow and encourage our sin to continue.
- Verse 2 – *we followed Satan in disobedience.* Behind the ways of the world there is mastermind, a real person who leads the rebellion against the Living God. His time is short and his defeat is already accomplished, yet his schemes and philosophy of selfishness control the 'ways of the world'. Far from being at the centre of God's purposes we served Satan's purposes. It is a sobering truth that beyond all the media, business and political powers of the age there is another, even more sinister, ruler who drives the 'ways of the world'. We so easily assume that we are 'good' if we don't harm others, if we keep to ourselves. Yet, the hours and years we waste away on our own pleasures are all part of Satan's vision. I might claim that I've never done anybody any harm today, but have I done anybody any good?
- Verse 3 – *we gratified the cravings of our flesh.* We spend our lives 'managing' our evil and selfish desires. Though we perhaps fought our gluttony, yet we indulge our pride or our love of popularity. Perhaps we serve others in our family, yet we have no time for others in need. Gratifying the cravings of our flesh conjures up the image of a desperate drug addict, whose mind is shut off to everything apart from getting another fix. We were like this with sin. Each sin corrupted us, leading us into worse and worse desires. We might have often regretted what we did. We might have been filled with self-loathing about the addictions that had mastered us, the angry temper that lurked within, the greed that festered in our hearts or the pride that made us look down on others. Yet, we were unable to escape these sins, constantly returning to them as a dog returns to its vomit (Proverbs 26:11). If ever we managed to get one

addiction under control, we simply ignored or expanded the other sins. Through it all there was an instinctive turning away from the LORD Jesus, the Light of the World.

- Verse 3 – *we were following the desires and thoughts of the flesh.* The 'flesh' is our fallen and corrupted human life. The natural tendencies of this flesh are to live as if there is no god, as if our immediate desires are all that really matter, as if I am the centre of the world. To look within, to go with our own instincts and desires sends us into ever deeper darkness and alienation from the Living God who is Spirit.
- Verse 3 – *we are natural objects of wrath.* With all this as our natural and 'normal' pattern of life and thought, then obviously we are naturally enemies of the Living God. We naturally constantly think and feel and act in ways that offend the holiness, goodness, love and glory of the Father, Son and Spirit. We provoke the anger of this majestic God, arrogantly and ignorantly carrying on this Satanic and fleshly rebellion in His wonderful creation.

In verses 1 – 3 the apostle Paul tells us plainly what we are outside of Christ. We were spiritually dead, utterly incapable of helping ourselves.

Our whole life was marked by disobedience. Whatever we did, no matter how good we thought it was, amounted to nothing more than "gratifying the cravings of our sinful nature and following its desires and thoughts."

> Of course, this does not mean that they were in all respects dead. It does not mean that they had no animal life, or that they did not breathe, and walk, and act. Nor can it mean that they had no living intellect or mental powers, which would not have been true. Nor does it settle any question as to their ability or power while in that state. It simply affirms a fact – that in relation to real spiritual life they were, in consequence of sin, like a dead man in regard to the objects which are around him. A corpse is insensible. It sees not, and hears not, and feels not. The sound of music, and the voice of friendship and of alarm, do not arouse it. The rose and the lily breath forth their fragrance around it, but the corpse perceives it not. The world is busy and active around it, but it is unconscious of it all. It sees no beauty in the

> landscape; hears not the voice of a friend; looks not upon the glorious sun and stars; and is unaffected by the running stream and the rolling ocean. So with the sinner in regard to the spiritual and eternal world, he sees no beauty in religion; he hears not the call of God; he is unaffected by the dying love of the Saviour; and he has no interest in eternal realities. In all these he feels no more concern, and sees no more beauty, than a dead man does in the world around him (Albert Barnes).

If we think of humanity as essentially good, then history will seem very frustrating and confusing. Why do we behave so badly even when circumstances are favourable, whether we are rich or poor? Why do we so easily use difficult times to excuse terrible behaviour? Why do we constantly invent myths and fables to bewitch our spirits? Why are we so dissatisfied with what we have?

These verses of Ephesians uncover the dark depths of the human condition. There is a heart of darkness within us and it cannot be illumined with any of our own powers of education, medicine or 'civilisation'.

BUT, verse 4, because of His love for us (in spite of His anger towards us), the Father gave us life and forgiveness, honour and glory in Christ. Why did He do this? Why did He make a Church out of such horrible material? We can see why He might elect and love *Jesus the Head* but not this Body of these sinful and selfish parts! It is "by grace you have been saved" – verse 5.

Grace is that free, undeserved friendship of the Living God. We cannot explain why the Father, Son and Spirit are so gracious, other than that is the character of their eternal life together. The one true God displays His uncreated and majestic glory, His great weight and substance, as He brings life and light to the evil dead like us.

Thinking back to Ephesians 1:13, we are struck by the fact that being included in Jesus is not a human achievement or the reward for religious or moral effort. As far from Him as we were, yet by grace through faith we were joined to Him even when we were at our very worst.

Speaking personally, Ephesians 1:13 with Ephesians 2:8 have been some of the most precious verses in the whole Bible to me. The plans and purposes of the Living God are clearly so marvellous and wise; His love is indescribable; the majesty and sacrifice of Jesus fills us with awe; the fact that the destiny of the Church was determined before the world began, underwritten by the purposes of the Almighty Father, is both comforting and exciting... and yet, where do I fit in? How can I also be included in Jesus? How can I become part of this Church that lives in Him? In my unbelief and doubt-filled thoughts I always imagine that it is impossible or too difficult or that I couldn't be welcome into such a glorious fellowship. Yet, when I turn to Ephesians 1:13 and then remember Ephesians 2:8 I am always amazed at how simple it is. To be included in Jesus has an infinite cost to Him, but to us there is no cost at all. We are included in Jesus when we hear about Him and trust Him.

2. By grace you have been saved – 2:6-10

The Church's connection with Jesus is incredible. All that has happened to Him, the Head, also happens to the Church, the Body.

His life is our life: the Church lives in Jesus – so, the fact that He has been raised above every possible opponent or power in the universe means that we have full and free access at all times into the intimate presence of the Most High God in the throne room of the universe – verse 6. As impossible as it sounds, given all the evil things we have done and said and desired, the Church rules with Jesus Christ in the highest heaven. This is why we know such joy and peace, such love and forgiveness in the Father's presence. This is why we experience the fruit and the gifts of the Spirit in the Church together. This is why even when we are rejected and killed for Jesus, the glory of God is displayed.

This is one of the deep truths we need to teach ourselves every day. The pagan world around us tells us (in many different ways) that we are unimportant specks in a random universe of chance and brutality; that there is no truth or goodness; that there is no heaven, no forgiveness, no Living God, no judgment day, no purpose. Yet, the truth is that simply by trusting Jesus we are reigning with Him in the highest heaven, in the fellowship of the Living God, looking forward to a day of liberation and justice when all things will be put right.

The religions, philosophies and lifestyles of the world around us (just like in Ephesus) will drag us back down into the darkness and depression, the confusion and chaos, if we allow those deceitful lies to rule over us. Each day we give thanks for the wonderful, gracious salvation that He has given to us in Jesus. We did not need to conceive it or achieve it – but simply to receive it.

Why did the Father allow the fullness of Jesus to extend to a Church made of people like us?

Verse 7 gives us the answer: simply so that we would be an everlasting testimony to His love and grace and kindness. When Paul speaks of "the coming ages" he may partly be thinking of the time in the new creation future when we are filled with amazement at our redemption, but more likely he is thinking of the ages of the world before that. Church history is filled with these wonderful examples and testimonies of the Father's goodness, given through Jesus by the power of the Spirit. When we want to see the reality of this grace we need only listen to the glorious stories of the local churches around the world and down through history. Even when massively outnumbered and living under oppressive regimes, yet the Church survives, displaying the wisdom and glory of the Living God.

The existence of the Church is totally due to the power and wisdom of God. Our survival is also a constant display of His power and glory.

We have become the Holy Body of Christ simply because we have trusted in Jesus. However, we cannot even congratulate ourselves on having done this – verse 8. On Judgment Day we will not be able to turn to the unbelievers and say "well, at least we were honest enough to recognize that we needed Jesus." No, our faith in Christ is itself a gift from God. Given our sin-addiction and slavery to Satan the only way any of us joined the Church was because the Father showed Jesus to us and drew us to trust in Him. Without the illuminating work of the Spirit, our blind eyes would never see the wonder and worth of Jesus.

Verse 9 is important. There can never be any boasting, pride or self-congratulation in the presence of God. This pride or boasting might be based on our religious faithfulness or zeal, but it may also be based on our self-improvement efforts. We can so easily give ourselves "marks out

of ten" for each day depending on whether we have done enough to earn the approval of God. This is a poisonous way to live, running directly against the way of Jesus. Every day, however much we do, however we have lived, we always come with entirely empty hands to our Father.

Verse 10 underlines this: we can never congratulate ourselves on living a good Christian life. It is not that once we were included in Christ we are now able to obey God in our own strength. No, even now we are always the workmanship of God. Our gracious Father has prepared whatever good things we ever accomplish for us in Jesus. Our life in Christ is grace from beginning to end.

Our existence as the Church is because of grace. We are God's workmanship.

The fact that each of us is included in the Church is in spite of us, not because of us.

This is such a liberating and comforting truth. Just as we could not save ourselves so we cannot preserve ourselves or produce the life of Jesus each day in our own power. If we entrust ourselves each day to the care and guidance of the Living God then we can rest assured that He will produce within us fruit for eternity.

We might think of the LORD God's power in terms of *creating* the universe, but *redeeming* the universe requires so very much more. One Puritan writer from the 17th century said that the only obstacle in the *creation* of the world was the creativity of the Father through the Son in the power of the Spirit – but, the *redemption* of the world presents a vast array of obstacles, any one of which seems impossible to overcome: sin, death, guilt, decay, shame, injustice, the devil, vanity, unbelief and selfishness.

Yes, the almighty power of the Living God is displayed in His gracious saving and preserving power. The glory of the Eternal God is displayed in His gracious workmanship, revealed by the good works He has prepared for us to do.

Study 2 Bible Questions

Ephesians 2:1-10

1. Verse 1 – What does Paul mean by the word 'dead'? How can people be 'dead' if they are also walking around, talking, alive and well?
2. Verse 2 – Many people want to drop out of society and escape the 'rat race'. Some even manage to live on a farm and provide for themselves. If we do this can we avoid the 'ways of this world' that Paul describes in verse 2?
3. Verse 3 – Sometimes the cravings of our sinful nature are very obvious: gluttony; lust; greed. How else do these cravings appear, in more subtle ways? What are the 'thoughts' of the sinful nature? What kind of thinking comes naturally to the sinful nature?
4. Verse 4 – If God is angry with us (verse 3b), then how can He also have 'great love' for us? What does this tell us about the Living God? Have we ever had an experience where love and anger for somebody all came together at once?
5. Verse 5 – How does the second part of verse 5 connect to the first part? Why does Paul conclude the verse with "it is by grace you have been saved"? How does the first part of the verse lead to that conclusion?
6. Verse 6 – Why was it so important for the Ephesians to know that they had been raised up to the highest heaven with Jesus? How does this verse have the same impact for us today? What are the claims and assumptions, the philosophies and myths that would threaten us in the world of today?
7. Verse 7 – How have the great riches of God's grace been shown through the Ephesian Church down through the ages? How can the life of our own local churches display these riches? Where is the kindness of God in Christ Jesus most clearly displayed?
8. Verse 8-9 – Why does Paul say that even coming to trust Jesus is a gift that God gives to us? We can see that saving ourselves is too much for us, but surely can't we trust and love Jesus no matter how messed up we are?

9. Verse 10 – Is there anything at all for us to do? If even faith is given to us, then shouldn't we do as little as possible to make sure that none of our works get in the way? Is it wrong to even speak about 'obeying the commands of God', because that might drive us into a 'works' way of thinking?

Study 2 Further Questions

1. When Paul describes us as "dead in our transgressions and sins", what does he mean by 'dead'? Do we still have the ability to search for God even before we are saved? Does the Spirit need to bring us to life first so that that we can then search for and find Christ? Or is the message of Christ, by the Spirit, powerful enough to make dead people hear and respond even as they are?
2. Could Paul really apply Ephesians 2:1-3 to a well-behaved, self-disciplined and friendly non-Christian? If we think about the best non-Christian people that we know, then how do these words apply to them? Are the ways of the world and the devil more subtle and clever than we assume? What are the cravings of the flesh that are most socially acceptable, that look the most respectable?
3. What actions can we take to sort ourselves out? Verses 4-10 emphasise all that the Father has done for us in Christ and how He does all this without any of our own action. Yet, when we are dealing with concrete problems of poverty, addiction, depression, greed, anger etc how does this confidence in the grace of God set us free to take real action? If we know that God is making everything work, can that give us confidence to work?

Study 2	Daily Readings
Day 1	Ephesians 2:1-3
Day 2	Romans 3:9-20
Day 3	Psalm 51
Day 4	Ephesians 2:4-10
Day 5	Romans 6:1-14
Day 6	Ezekiel 37:1-14
Day 7	John 3:1-21

The daily Bible readings are an opportunity not only to read through all of the material in the book under study, but also to read parts of the Bible that relate to the themes and issues that we have been considering. We try to make sure that we receive light from the whole Bible as we think through the key issues each week.

Study 3: The Church is one family Ephesians 2:11-3:13

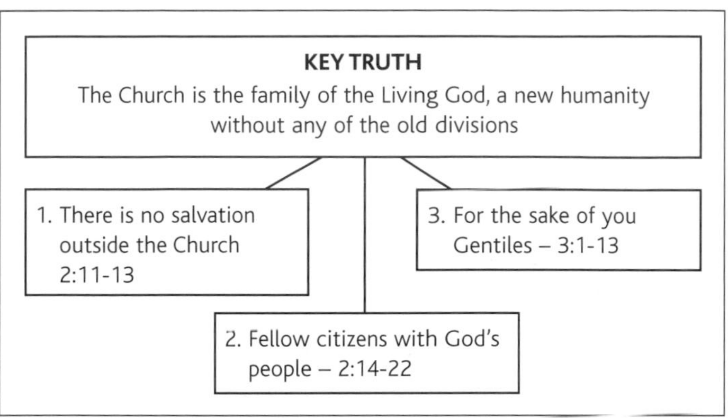

1. There is no salvation outside the Church – 2:11-13

Having considered how lost we are – dead in sins, enslaved to evil desires and serving the devil's schemes – Paul looks at that same situation on a global scale, in terms of the nations and religions of the world.

We are not isolated individuals, all choosing our own path through life. In reality we are locked into religions, philosophies, traditions and nations that control the way we think and act. Even though Christ and His gospel are proclaimed in the stars, the hills, the plants, the weather and the animals, in so many marvellous ways, yet this great sermon of creation cannot be heard when our seeing and hearing is directed and distorted by the "principalities and powers" (not to mention the darkness that is within our own heart and mind).

The Ephesian people were at the centre of a vast religious cult focussed on Artemis. The temple that dominated their skyline also dominated their assumptions and experience. The Living God who made the heavens and the earth was known to His Church in Israel but unknown and inaccessible to the ordinary Ephesians.

The community of Christ, the Church of the Living God, had been enclosed by a boundary since the time of Abraham – the boundary of circumcision (Ephesians 2:11 and see Genesis 17). The Church was further contained and defined within a specific geographical area by the Law given through Moses. Inside that "wall of separation" the Church community had the covenant promises of the Living God: the prophecies of Christ; the presence of the Spirit; the assurances of hope; the experience of joy, peace, love and worship (Ephesians 2:12).

Outside the 'wall of separation' the nations of the wall were lost in the terrible darkness of being "separate from Christ, excluded from citizenship in Israel and foreigners to the covenants of the promise, without hope and without God in the world".

I imagine what it would have been like to live where I do now in North West England 3,000 years ago. Pagan religion dominated northern Europe and whatever remnants of the faith of Noah might have been left in the nations of the world were totally corrupted and confused. Perhaps leaders from this country went to hear of the Living God from Solomon (as described in 1 Kings 10:23-24), but otherwise it is hard to see how anyone could have ever even heard of the Church let alone be joined to it.

A wonderful change came about through the death, resurrection and ascension of Jesus. He had made a promise to Abraham long ago that through the Church community blessing would go out to all the nations of the world (Genesis 12:1-3). Through His great work, Jesus not only accomplished the mighty work of atonement for the world, but also brought the Law to an end. He knocked down that boundary wall that had temporarily separated the circumcised people from the uncircumcised people; the Jews from the Gentiles. It was as if the Church had been dammed up by the Law in one specific place and then as the wall of separation fell down so Israel spread out across the whole world, taking in Gentiles along with the Jews regardless of their background or status under the Law.

I can now be British *and* a member of the Body of Christ. Have you ever wondered what is the difference between the Old Testament and the New Testament? Yes, the Old Testament Church looked *forward* to the work of Christ and the New Testament Church looks *back* to the work of Christ, yet when we read the book of Acts or the New Testament epistles how is the difference primarily represented? Both Old Testament and New Testament saints are saved by the same gospel, the same Saviour. We enjoy the presence of the same Holy Spirit. We experience the same Christian life. Yet, *then* the only way that anyone in the world could find peace with God was by renouncing their nationality and travelling to Israel to become a Jew.

The blood of Jesus brought near those who were far away from the life of God (Ephesians 2:13).

How did His blood do this? How could the blood of a man make such a profound change in the eternal destiny of humanity? Isn't this just some strange remnant from an ancient primitive religion?

In the modern world we all too easily reduce 'sin' to mere psychological terms. In an almost instinctive way we think of sin as 'letting ourselves down' or 'failing to live up to our standards' or 'missing our full potential'. In other words we easily reduce sin to an issue of personal development or personal well-being. However, although the Bible acknowledges the way that sin really does cause deep harm, confusion and corruption to us, yet that is only a secondary by-product of what sin really is. There are two dominant ideas in the Bible's teaching about sin, contained in its two most common words: sins and transgressions. On the one hand we deliberately do things that are against the laws and character of the Living God: we act in defiance or rebellion against Him. On the other hand we fail to live as we were designed to do: we do not live up to God's glory, the standard that is the basic requirement of our life. We were created to live as manifestations of God's glory, creatures who live *out* and fellowship *in* that glorious life of the Father, Son and Holy Spirit. Even when we are not deliberately breaking His commands, we constantly fall short of this glory, wasting our lives on worthless 'empty glory'.

So, whether we think of our wilful acts of rebellion or our constant failure to live out the glory of God, we have forfeited our very lives. From the very beginning of the Bible and repeated in so many ways all the way through, we are taught over and over again that our sins and transgressions carry the penalty of death. Though we were made to live forever, as an entire race we are condemned to die and be eternally excluded, thrown out into that outer darkness forever. There simply is no place for us at all in God's world because of what we are and what we do. In fact, it is not just that we are useless to the great purposes of this Living God, but even worse our sins and transgressions provoke Him to anger: we offend Him by our godless ways and He looks forward to that day when He can purge the world of all this evil.

Yes, those pagan nations may have imagined all kinds of ideas about living on beyond death (whether the natural immortality of the soul from the Greek philosophers; the halls of Valhalla from the Norse; the cycle of rebirth in Hinduism etc), yet the Bible clearly states that without Christ there is no hope beyond death; no life other than the ghastly existence of burning shame and angry bitterness of Hell itself.

So, how can there be good news when the situation is so utterly hopeless?

Throughout the Hebrew Scriptures, time after time, the anger and judgment of God is averted through blood sacrifice – see especially the Passover of Exodus 12. It was as if the need to throw us out of life was satisfied by the death of the animal. That animal, which had done no wrong, would stand in for the human sinner and its blood would cry out that the sins and transgressions had been punished, that death had taken them away. Of course, the blood of mere animals couldn't really satisfy the heart of the Living God, yet all the time that animal blood was prophesying of some other blood that really could pay the price of sin and wash away our transgressions.

The Living God still loves us, in spite of all our sin and transgressions. His love for us is impossible to explain and yet He loved us so much that He became one of us, a real human being, to create a way back. He came and lived our life as it was supposed to be lived – free from all rebellion and always living up to the great glory of God. He really did display the glory and majesty, the love and truth, the justice and compassion of the Living God in every aspect of His life. Having established a human life that was worthy of life, He then took our condemned human life with all our sins and transgressions as His own. He became sin on the Cross and felt the full force of being alienated from God in death. Yes, we might wonder how the One Living God could do this within Himself: how could the eternal Father and the eternal Son be alienated from each other yet be also working together in the deepest sense? We stand in awe and worship before such mysteries, yet we know them to be true.

Within the heart of the Living God, at the very centre of the life of the Father, Son and Spirit, there was what can only be thought of in terms of a mysterious and profound conflict. His hatred of what we do and say could not be forgotten no matter how much He also loved us. How could He express and satisfy that hatred and anger against our evil whilst at the same time keeping us alive, holding onto us, redeeming us from our own crimes?

When the blood of God was shed on the Cross; as His blood poured out of His body; as He cried out in the depths of alienation from His Father – "My God, My God, why have You forsaken Me?" – that blood was the proof and the power of that satisfaction. The heart of the Living God was satisfied by that sacrifice and blood. When He looks at our sins and transgressions He can also look at that blood of the Cross and be satisfied that it has all been confronted and condemned, as it needs to be.

No matter how far from God anyone ever is, the blood of Jesus can satisfy the heart of God and bring us near to Him.

"In Christ Jesus you who once were far off have been brought near by the blood of Christ."

The Church of Jesus Christ has spread out to the whole world, to the deepest and darkest places of paganism, atheism and superstition, to bring the warmth and welcome of God's own family.

We need to remember this when people are cynical about the Church. For all its many faults, nevertheless, no Christian can cut themselves off from the Church. There is no salvation outside the Church. It is impossible to be a solitary Christian.

2. Fellow citizens with God's people – 2:14-22

Up to now Paul has been describing the Church as the Body of Christ – or simply as those who are *in Christ*. We are united to Christ such that our sinful lives have been taken by Him and all His righteousness and riches have been given to us. But, now, halfway through Ephesians chapter 2 and into chapter 3, Paul moves on to a different way of describing the Church – the new humanity.

The Church is the Holy Temple of God, the household of God, a new humanity.

Look at verses 14-16 – Jesus "Himself is our peace, who has made the two one and has destroyed the barrier, the dividing wall of hostility. His purpose was to create in Himself one new man (a new humanity) out of the two, thus making peace, and in this one body to reconcile both of them to God through the cross, by which He put to death their hostility."

Jesus has created a new humanity in which the whole world can be reconciled to God through the Cross. A new humanity: this is yet another way of describing the Church.

As we look at our world today, there can be no answer apart from the formation of a new human race. The old human race with its addiction to conflict, greed and lust provokes constant conflicts and division.

In this old human race the divisions go deep and roll on for generation after generation. The origins of our divisions are sometimes lost in the mists of time, whereas others are kept all too fresh and raw by renewed hostilities and offences.

Paul thinks especially of that deepest division between the Jews and Gentiles; Israel and the pagan nations of the world. How could there be blessing for all the nations of the world when they were defined as cut off, shut out, without God and without hope?

Only Christ's new humanity, which is the Church, can look forward to a world in which weapons are made into farming equipment.

In verses 17 and 18 we discover a tremendous comfort. Jesus has not left it up to us to bring our divided world into the Church. When we do our evangelism, no matter how poor at it we are, it is Jesus Himself who is the real evangelist. He preaches to the divided and separated world, through us. We need to appreciate that. Think of someone to whom we have been trying to witness. Wouldn't it be great if we could take a great and famous evangelist like Billy Graham or even the apostle Paul with us every time we tried to present the gospel to them? Yet, we have an infinitely better evangelist going with us all the time.

When we tell others about Jesus, then ultimately it is Jesus Himself who is preaching to the world. In one sense we do not need to worry too much about our techniques, methods and strategies because Jesus Himself will preach through us if we are focussed on Him and working for His glory.

A Christian friend recently spoke about meeting a woman in a café each week where they would chat about life. The Christian would bring a truth about Jesus from the Bible each week to share and the woman eventually started coming to Church and met Jesus for herself. Later she said that it was as if God Himself were speaking to her each week as the Bible truth was shared: as if the message was meant just for her. This is what it can be like as we also share the glory of Jesus with those around us. Christ will come and preach peace to those who are far from God.

Throughout the first three chapters of Ephesians we seem to be stowaways, non-contributing passengers, in the Church as the Father, Son and Spirit do all the work.

Jesus Himself preaches and the Spirit brings people to the Father (verse 18). Through Jesus the whole world can come to the Father in the power of the Spirit. Whether we were Jews, Muslims, atheists, Buddhists, Church-goers, agnostics, Hindus, communists or pagans, all of us may join together in Jesus and by the Spirit have genuine communion with the Most High God the Father.

So, verse 19, no matter how messed up or far away we were, through Jesus we are true members of Israel, part of the covenant community, circumcised in the heart by Christ Himself. By trusting Jesus we are citizens of God's kingdom just as much as Moses, Abraham, Isaiah, David or even Jesus Himself.

God's family is like a cosmic, holy temple for God to live in (verses 21-22). The whole 'building' is made up of the whole variety of human beings from all over the world built on and supported by Jesus Christ Himself. We may have tried to find 'god' or 'meaning' or 'truth' in all our different religions, philosophies and cultures yet in this united, multi-coloured temple we become the dwelling-place of the Living God.

The entire universe is not an adequate 'container' for the supreme majesty of the Living God. In 2 Chronicles 6:18, when Solomon built his amazing temple for the Angel of the LORD, he said "will God really dwell on earth with men? The heavens, even the highest heavens, cannot contain you. How much less this temple I have built!" Yet, Christ Himself is the builder of a temple where the whole Trinity dwells forever and ever: the temple of the Church; the united community of Christ's people from every tribe, nation, language and continent.

3. For the sake of you Gentiles – 3:1-13

Paul is about to explain why he is prepared to be thrown in prison so that the Church may go out to all the Gentile nations of the world. He does not want the Ephesians to be discouraged when they hear about all his sufferings (3:13) because these sufferings are actually being used to bring the reality of Christ to more and more people. Yet, as he starts (verse 1) he realises that he needs to explain further about this special work that he has been given.

Paul explains that he was given a special commission by Jesus Himself to go to the 'Gentiles' (the non-Jewish people of the world) in order to bring this great news of joining in the family of God through Jesus.

Now, of course, this had been spoken about since the beginning of the Hebrew Scriptures. Abraham was a Gentile before his circumcision and Christ had promised Abraham that all the nations of the world would be blessed through the promised Seed (Christ Himself). People from many outside nations joined Israel in the great exodus from Egypt and when we read the life of David we are always amazed at how many Philistines and Hittites had been won to Christ through his life and witness. The prophets constantly deliver messages about and to the surrounding nations, showing how much the LORD God was interested in them.

Yet, in all these examples, the nations were required to renounce their own nationality to join Israel: they had to become circumcised Israelites

and cease to be Egyptians, Babylonians, Greeks, Romans, Syrians etc.

So, the ancient Church always knew that Christ was winning all the nations to Himself, but the idea that these nations would remain Gentile and yet be part of Israel, included in God's family, was something that was not revealed in the Hebrew Scriptures as it was revealed through the apostles. This seems to be a very big claim by the apostle Paul! How could the apostles ever go beyond the ancient Law and prophets in any way! It sounds almost like heresy. Yet, as we have seen, the truth itself was not a new truth: the salvation of the Gentiles had been known and practiced since the very beginning. The way this would be worked out on a global scale was not revealed so clearly before. Paul actually says (verse 9) that it was the 'administration' (the practical outworking) of this mystery that was kept hidden in God for long ages. The most ancient Law and prophets had promised that the Church would cover all the nations of the world... but how could that be done under the Law when people had to travel so far to come to Jerusalem for the feasts and sacrifices? The Living God who made all things had prepared and planned for the global Israel long before He explained the details of its administration.

This was the biggest debate and controversy in the New Testament – precisely because this was the one 'new' thing. Even the great apostle Peter had to be challenged by Paul to live consistently with this (see Galatians 2:11-14).

Through the gospel the Gentiles are heirs together with Israel – members together of one body in Jesus.

One preacher puts it like this: "Pentecost is not the birth of the Church, but it is the re-formation of the Church. Now, people from all over the world form the one Body of Christ – and they stay right where they are. There is no need to immigrate to Israel. Christ sanctifies every race, every nation, every culture. In many churches we see this multi-national truth at every meeting. In some city centre churches the whole world seems to be represented – and this is what makes it such a powerful testimony to this great truth of the Body of Christ. The world today is wracked with ethnic conflict. The United Nations is not the remedy, because the world's ethnic conflicts simply get played out at the UN. No, in only one body in the world is ethnic division irrelevant – and that is the Body of Christ."

There is just one more thing we must notice about the Church from chapter 3. No matter how despised or disregarded the Church is by the world, yet there is one group of authorities who are well aware of the Church's importance.

No matter how big or small the human congregation of the Church is, yet there is another audience paying attention to the Church. Look at verse 10 – "The Father's intent was that now, through the Church, the manifold wisdom of God should be made known to the rulers and authorities in the heavenly realms, according to his eternal purpose which he accomplished in Christ Jesus our Lord."

The rulers and authorities in the heavenly realms! The Bible doesn't want us to become distracted by or obsessed with these spiritual beings so they are never given a systematic treatment in the Bible. It is enough for us to know that the creation has two aspects, as we say in the opening part of the Creed – a visible and an invisible. The invisible creation is populated by angelic and demonic beings who have authority over the visible world. These invisible beings understand much of the nature of the Church and pay very careful attention to us. Yet, they are not all-wise or all-knowing. The Church is their school where they can learn about the manifold wisdom and the eternal purposes of God. As we live out the way of Jesus in our day to day lives, we are presenting the hidden mysteries of the Living God to this unseen audience. When we gather together to study the Scriptures, to worship God, and to apply the gospel to our lives, we are handling profound mysteries into which the angels long to look. The Church, by the grace of God, is the Teacher to these rulers and authorities in the heavenly realms.

It is good that Paul doesn't go into this in too much detail or else we would perhaps become fascinated in an unhealthy and unhelpful way with it all. Yet, he tells us enough to make us take our life as the Church very seriously. It is the Father's intention that the world of angels and demons learn about Him through the Church.

Study 3 Bible Questions

Ephesians 3:1-13

1. Verse 1 – Why does Paul describe himself as a 'prisoner' of Jesus Christ? What does this tell us about his life and mission?
2. Verses 2-3 – Paul assumes they have already heard his testimony about how Jesus confronted him and sent him off to the non-Jewish world. Why does he want to remind them of this and the fact that the 'mystery' or 'secret' was made known to him by personal revelation?
3. Verses 4-6 – Three times in these verses Paul speaks of a 'mystery'. In English a 'mystery' is something that we can't understand, but in Greek it is a 'secret' that has become known. However, Paul just tells us in simple language what this 'secret' is in verse 6. How does this 'secret' explain some of the biggest confrontations in the life of Paul? Does this 'secret' help us to understand the book of Acts?
4. Verses 4-6 – If Paul's life has been shaped by this 'secret', how does verse 1 connect to verse 5?
5. Whenever Paul writes about the salvation of the Gentiles, he keeps going back to the ancient Hebrew Scriptures: to Moses, the Prophets and the Psalms – see for example, Romans 9:24-29 and Romans 15:7-12.So, what does Paul mean by verse 5?
6. Verses 7-8 – How would we describe Paul's charismatic gift from God?
7. Verse 9 – If the secret is "Jews and Gentiles joined together as one body in Jesus Christ", then why was the administration of this kept hidden for such long ages? Why does Paul remind us that God created all things?
8. Verse 10-11 – Why must the unified Body of Christ be displayed to the whole world, in every nation? Why is it so important that the united, loving Body of Jesus be displayed so clearly?
9. Verses 12-13 – What was the value of Paul's sufferings? Why did he keep on serving and speaking even when it got him in so much trouble? What will we do that would bring the same glory, even if it also brings the same sufferings?

Study 3 Further Questions

1. The terrible and terrifying state of the world outside the Church needs to be taken seriously. It is all too common for Bible readers to try to minimise the meaning of Ephesians 2:12. Nevertheless, we dare not do that, for the sake of Christ's glory and the eternal safety of our fellow human beings. Think of the saints down through history who have travelled to the most difficult and dangerous places so that others may know the glory of Christ and find in Him eternal safety. Yet, today, we do not need to travel anywhere to meet people who are utterly lost in darkness, sin and ignorance – alienated from God and without hope. What does all this mean for our witness to the way of Jesus?

2. Some Christians believe that the LORD God has a different plan for Jewish people than Gentile people. They believe that the racial or genetic history of a person determines where they stand in God's plans. Some even go so far as to suggest that Jewish people are saved without trusting in Jesus! These kinds of ideas have often come from Gentiles too who have also believed that their genetic heritage or family heritage sets them apart from the rest of humanity. How does Paul address these ideas? Is a Jewish person saved in a different way to a Gentile person?

Study 3 Daily Readings

Day 1	Ephesians 2:11-22
Day 2	Ephesians 3:1-13
Day 3	Romans 16:17-27
Day 4	Colossians 1:21-29
Day 5	Genesis 12:1-9
Day 6	Isaiah 52:7-15
Day 7	Revelation 21:22-22:6

The daily Bible readings are an opportunity not only to read through all of the material in the book under study, but also to read parts of the Bible that relate to the themes and issues that we have been considering. Wetry to make sure that we receive light from the whole Bible as we think through the key issues each week.

Study 4: The Church is equipped by Jesus Ephesians 3:14-4:16

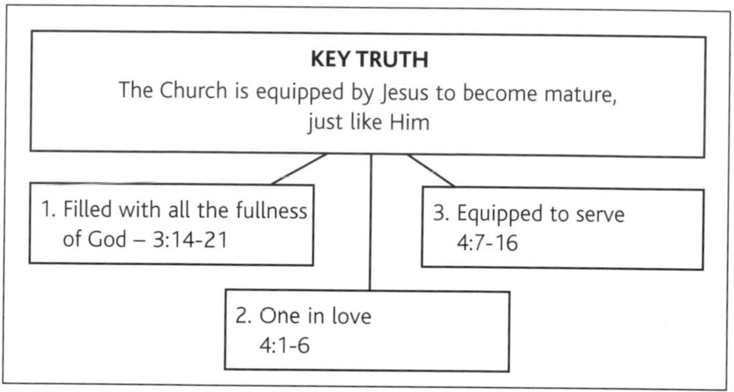

1. Filled with all the fullness of God – 3:14-21

Paul left us with a vision of the plans of God spanning all of history and all of the world, displayed to the invisible creatures of the heavenly realms as the definitive presentation of the Father's wonderful wisdom. Building a global Church, filled with all the many varieties of human culture and language, is at the very centre of the deep and eternal plans of the Father, Son and Spirit.

So then Paul has tremendous confidence in praying for the Church. The Living God has given His all for the Church, even to the point of pouring out His own blood to create this new humanity for Him to live forever. If that is true, then all the very richest treasures will be given to us in prayer.

Paul kneels down to pray indicating his zeal and humility in prayer (verse 14). Kneeling seems to be the right way for us to pray and it is hard to ever justify the slouched attitude that is sometimes seen. It is well worth spending time looking up the following references to posture in prayer: 2 Chronicles 6:13; Isaiah 45:23; Philippians 2:10; Romans 14:11; Ezra 9:5; Nehemiah 8:6; 2 Chronicles 7:3; 2 Chronicles 29:20 and 29; Psalms 5:7; 132:7; 138:2; Luke 22:41; Acts 7:60; 20:36; 21:5.

There is a question about the translation and meaning of verse 14. The NIV translation sees the verse as referring to the Father's name being given to the whole global Church family.

> The dominant theme of these chapters is that through Christ the 'one God and Father of us all' (4:6) has only one family or household to which Jewish and Gentile believers equally belong. It seems better, therefore, to translate pasa patria 'the whole family' (AV), 'his whole family' (NEB margin) or 'the whole family of believers' (NIV). Then the addition of the words in heaven and on earth will indicate that the Church militant on earth and the Church triumphant in heaven, though separated by death, are nevertheless only two parts of the one great family of God.[8]

On the other hand the NIV also has a footnote to mark the other possibility – "For this reason I kneel before the Father, from whom *all fatherhood* in heaven and on earth derives its name." The ESV Bible translation puts verse 15 like this – "from whom every family in heaven and earth is named".

If this is correct then Paul is reminding us how everything in the whole creation is not only created by the Father but is defined by Him. The life of the Trinity is reflected in all kinds of family relationships all over the whole creation. Sometimes critics suggest that 'religious people' project their own experiences of life into an imaginary heaven or onto an imaginary 'god', defining 'god' according to the kind of things they see around them. However, with this telling phrase, Paul reminds us that in fact the whole creation is a projection of the life and mind of the Living God! We are derived from Him, not the other way around.

With this big view of the Father over the heavens and the earth Paul prays for the Ephesian Church living in the shadow of that huge pagan temple.

Paul's pray begins with the 'glorious riches' of the Father – or perhaps 'the riches of His glory'. The overflowing and wonderful life of the Father is the basis for everything in heaven and on earth. Every good gift comes from

8 Stott, J. R. W. (1979). *God's new society: The message of Ephesians* (133). Downers Grove, Ill.: InterVarsity Press.

our heavenly Father and there is no limit to what He can do or give. Our prayers are never too much for our generous Father: our prayers are always too little, perhaps as we ask for things that are nothing but the selfish desires of our flesh (James 4:3). That Ephesian Church may have had little political power and small financial resources, yet the true riches of the Father meant that they out-loved, out thought and outlived the cult of Artemis.

If we are prepared to pray these big prayers for the revolution of Jesus, then we must also be ready for the action and the sacrifice that these big prayers will bring. The glorious riches of the Father show up the worthless 'treasures' of this passing age and bring that revolution into our own hearts and lives.

There are two requests made from the glorious riches of the Father: strength and Christ Himself.

First, Paul prays that the Father would "strengthen you with power through His Spirit in your inner humanity" (verse 16). Clearly the Ephesians felt weak and Paul knew that they needed that mighty energy of the Holy Spirit. When we read Acts 19 we see all kinds of power at work in Ephesus, from the magical power of the sorcerers to the financial power of the metalworkers and the mob power of the citizens. Yet, the power of the Spirit had been shown through the apostles (Acts 19:6 and 11-12). The Ephesians needed more than apostolic miracles though: they also needed the constant strength to think and act like Jesus Christ in all the challenges and opportunities of day-to-day discipleship. The real power of the Spirit is shown when sinners are transformed into saints who have taken off that old humanity and put on the new humanity of Jesus Himself. When we see people living with the same kind of love and holiness that Jesus Himself showed then we know that the Holy Spirit of the Living God is with us. Jesus Himself taught that the world will believe when they see how we obey Him and love each other.

Second, the strength is needed so that "Christ may dwell in your hearts through faith" (verse 17). To know the presence of Jesus with us is surely the greatest assurance and experience that we can ever know: we can face anything if we know that He is living within us. Yet, according to

Paul, for this to happen we must have strength "with power through His Spirit in your inner humanity". Throughout this letter Paul is encouraging the Ephesians to keep their hearts, minds and lives centred on Jesus. If they are dragged away by the unbelieving ideas and lifestyles around them then they will be ineffective, confused, depressed and fearful. Instead, as the Church puts on the mind and life of Christ, following His ways in simple trust and love, so the Church also experiences the presence of Jesus Himself, living within us.

Chapter 1 told us that we are 'in Christ' when we trusted Him and that is the very foundation and core of our salvation. We are joined to Christ, clothed in His righteousness with our sins forgiven by grace alone through faith alone. Yet, Paul is addressing the consequences of this gracious status for the Ephesian Christians.

The objective truth is that they are 'in Christ' but what of the subjective truth of 'Christ in them'?

Trusting Jesus is not something that is done once and then forgotten: it is the essence of the Christian life each and every day. Every day we trust Jesus and follow Him. Every day the temptation is to trust in our own resources and wisdom, to follow our own desires and listen to the unbelieving voices around us and within. The truth of our status in Jesus must be owned and lived each day.

The Ephesians needed the strength of the power of the Spirit in their inner humanity so that they would stand firm in trusting Jesus and thus know His abiding presence with them. Notice that Christ lives in their inner human life 'by faith' (verse 17). Trusting Jesus on the one hand or unbelief on the other hand are always the explanation for the way we live, for good or ill.

In John 14:23 Jesus said "If anyone loves me, he will obey my teaching. My Father will love him, and we will come to him and make our home with him."

Again, in Revelation 3:20 Jesus issues an invitation to His Church – "I stand at the door and knock. If anyone hears my voice and opens the door, I will come in and eat with him, and he with me."

We trust Jesus and therefore we daily trust in His teaching and His commands. We daily conform our minds to His truth and daily say 'no' to the futile thinking and selfish cravings of our old human nature. As we do this so we experience the reality and presence of Jesus among us.

The "inner humanity" seems to stand in contrast to our outer life; the life of our heart and mind as opposed to the life of our flesh. We might outwardly be wasting away, but inwardly renewed day by day to become more and more like Jesus (see 2 Corinthians 4:16-18). Looking at us in a scientific laboratory that new humanity of Jesus could not be detected, but it is more real, more substantial and everlasting than this passing flesh. It is important to daily state the truth of this. If we get hypnotised by the immediate and surface world around us we will quickly lose sight of reality: by listening to the pagan culture around us or even to the cravings of our flesh, we will fall into the thinking, feeling and behaviour of that old humanity.

Remember that Paul is writing to Christian people. The daily battle for the heart and mind goes on until we see Jesus face to face.

The immediate fruit of Christ living in us is "being rooted and established in love" – and from this deep foundation of love Paul prays that the Ephesians would *together* grasp the love of Jesus in every dimension. Rooted like a plant and founded like a building, the Church is to have love at the very depths of her life. We might know all kinds of truth and have stood firmly in many conflicts; our preaching might be courageous and clear; we might be ready to challenge all the assumptions of the age; yet, what is the point of any of these things if we are not a community of genuine, practical, sincere love? What happens between our meetings? Are the sick visited and the elderly cared for? Are the single parents supported and the lonely invited to our homes? Are the anxious comforted and the hungry fed? If we just pay others to do these things or we assume 'this isn't my ministry' then can we ever claim to be rooted and founded in love?

As we trust Jesus so we live out His Way; as we live out His Way so we experience His indwelling presence and love among us.

Paul prays that the Ephesians would know this love not simply as a historical fact but as a contemporary experience: that they would "know this love that surpasses knowledge". The love of Jesus will not only stretch our thinking but also our feeling and doing. Not only in the three dimensions of the world around us (wide, long and high) but also in another dimension of 'depth', the love of Jesus takes us into levels of reality that far surpass all that we think or imagine. Why or how? How or why does the love of Jesus carry us so high and so deep, far beyond all the scientific formulas, the philosophical principles and the theological debates?

Paul explains that if we know this love that surpasses knowledge then we are "filled to the measure of all the fullness of God".

Human religion and human philosophy have all kinds of ideas about 'god' and 'reality'. Generally their highest thoughts are to do with 'forces' or impersonal 'essence'. For example, when the famous philosopher Rene Descartes (1596-1650) was trying to prove the existence of his god he defined him/her/it in this way: "By 'God', I understand, a substance which is infinite, independent, supremely intelligent, supremely powerful, and which created both myself and everything else... that exists."

The apostle Peter stated that it is through Jesus that we believe in the Living God (1 Peter 1:21). The Living God is so utterly different – wholly other. In our fallen sinful confusion we tend to fragment into impersonal ways of thinking and living. Our hearts become hard and selfish; our thoughts are abstract and disconnected; our lives are compartmentalised and enslaved to habits, desires and fears. Yet, the Living God is the Father, Son and Holy Spirit, eternally united in love and fellowship. When we are drawn into the life of God through our loving Church fellowship then we are finding the true centre of the universe, the doors of perception are opened and the universe makes sense.

Sometimes human religions imagine a single god who is just one single 'person' and then they struggle to find any place for love with such a strange god. Other human religions seem to grasp that the 'divine' is multi-personal, but invent all kinds of separate 'gods' and cannot see how it all fits together. Yet, in Jesus alone we are shown the only Living God who is the Father, Son and Holy Spirit one in life and love.

So, our goal is not simply to *think* about or *observe* the 'fullness of God' but for us also to be filled with this divine fullness. Christ is Himself the full and total expression of the 'fullness of God': He is the highest and deepest expression of the life of God. Jesus is God at full strength (Colossians 2:9). As we too are caught up into the life and love of Christ Jesus, as our Church fellowships conform to His Way of love, then we too participate in the divine nature, looking on into a future of constant growth into the very fullness of the Living God.

> God's fullness or perfection becomes the standard or level up to which we pray to be filled. The aspiration is the same in principle as that implied by the commands to be holy as God is holy, and to be perfect as our heavenly Father is perfect.[9]

So, if the One, Eternal Living God has determined that His Church be filled to the full measure with His own life of love, then our prayer meetings must be times of intense excitement and wonder: He can always do far more than we can ask or even imagine. He displays His glory and wisdom through the Church so we need only present Him with opportunities to do this.

When our prayers are essentially "make my/our life easier or make us more popular..." then we should not be surprised that we are not heard. When we turn away from His life of love for our own selfish desires (no matter how well disguised they are under our 'religious' language), He will not listen to us. Yet, when we are captivated by His glory, laying down our lives in love for each other, we cannot imagine what He will do with our local Church!

2. One in love – 4:1-6

Having prayed for the unimaginable goal of being filled with the maximum of the divine life and having asked to know the unknowable love of Jesus, Paul gets right into describing what all this looks like on the

9 Stott, J. R. W. (1979). *God's new society: The message of Ephesians* (138). Downers Grove, Ill.: InterVarsity Press.

ground in our day to day life. If we have such a very high and cosmic insight into the very centre of all reality, into the depths of the Living God, we must "live a life worthy of the calling" (verse 1).

What does the fullness of God look like when a local Church is filled with the presence of God?

> Be completely humble and gentle; be patient, bearing with one another in love. Make every effort to keep the unity of the Spirit through the bond of peace.

The Father and Son have been united in loving fellowship together in the unity of the Spirit for infinite ages before the universe ever existed. This is the life that the Living God shares with us in Christ. The fruit of trusting Jesus is this life growing up in the local Church. The real test of our maturity and knowledge is how we treat one another. How are the weakest people treated in our local Church family? How much patience and love is shown to those we find hard to deal with?

There are so many attacks on the unity of our local Church, from within and without. We will have all kinds of different views of so many subjects; we have different ideas about what needs to be done; we are all still living with our old humanity with all its pride, anger, impatience, selfishness and greed; Satan and his agents will sow weeds of division, lies and grumbling; and the pressures of the world create further tension among us. Yet, if our roots and foundations are set in the Way of Jesus, in His Way of love, then we really can "make every effort to keep the unity of the Spirit in the bond of peace".

Yes, our leaders need to challenge us and make decisions we might find hard or even put out of the fellowship those who will not repent, but we constantly put aside our own interests and ideas, making every effort to stay united in love and peace in Spirit. It is so easy to indulge our grumbling or stir up division with our 'concerns', yet true spiritual maturity is revealed when we put the interests of the Church family ahead of our own, praying to the Father "not my will, but yours be done."

In verses 4-6 notice how often the word 'one' occurs: *one* body; *one* Spirit; *one* hope; *one* Lord; *one* faith; *one* baptism; *one* God and Father.

Unity is absolutely central here. Our sinful human nature always wants to divide, to be different, to be 'number one', to 'get our concerns off our chest', to make sure 'people know what my view is' etc. We like to be part of an 'inner group', part of the elite group that has deeper wisdom, understanding, courage, truth, practical work than everybody else in the Church family. Our flesh always cries out to be recognised by others for our work, our abilities, the fact that we knew something before anybody else. Yet, against this divisive and rotten human nature, the Way of the Father, Son and Holy Spirit is unity. We are one body, a united Church family, bound together by the same Holy Spirit who is within us all. We have the same hope of the glory of God in the new creation. We trust in the same LORD Jesus who died for us all and calls everyone of us to follow Him in the same Way, Truth and Life. Since the beginning of the world there has only ever been one faith: faith in the LORD Jesus Christ. We are baptised into that one body of the Church – and it does not matter who baptised us or what method was used or how much water there was, only that we were baptised in the name of the Father, Son and Holy Spirit as disciples of that one LORD Jesus. God the Father, is the source of it all: He sent that one LORD Jesus and sends the one Spirit through Jesus to build that one Church. We all come to the same heavenly Father every day and He provides for us all with the same generous love and care.

It is as if we need to daily remind ourselves of this great unity of the Spirit through the one LORD Jesus in the one Heavenly Father. When we are meeting together as the local Church family, before we ever say a word we need to run through Ephesians 4:4-6 in our hearts and minds to kill off those weeds of division that will constantly spring up.

If the Church plant is rooted in love and we weed out these seeds of division, then we can grow up into that united love of the fullness of God.

3. Equipped to serve – 4:7-16

It is this growth into maturity that Paul addresses next. If we are standing on a firm foundation of love and unity, then the one Body of the local Church can function and grow into strength and maturity.

There is no room for self-serving in the Church – no room for pride or bullying. Whatever a person was outside Christ, whether they were highly esteemed or utterly despised, yet here, in the Church, we are one, members of each other. We should spare no effort, no inconvenience in order to maintain and manifest this glorious reality. Chapter 4 of Ephesians, in fact, right down into chapter 5, is jam packed full of instructions on how we can grow up together as a Body in unity and love.

We are not naturally equipped to behave like this. Paul has told us that naturally we crave to indulge our own sinful natures. However, verse 7 – "to each one of us grace has been given as Christ apportioned it." Each member in the unity of the Spirit is given that free friendship (grace) from Jesus Christ so that we can play a part in building up the local Church family into that fullness of God.

Paul teaches us the significance of Christ's ascension for the life of the Church. When Christ ascended He took the whole creation captive to Himself. Everything in the universe belongs to Christ to administer as He sees fit. Okay, so what does He do with all these resources? Verse 11 – "It was he who gave some to be apostles, some to be prophets, some to be evangelists, and some to be pastors and teachers, to prepare God's people for works of service, so that the body of Christ may be built up until we all reach unity in the faith and in the knowledge of the Son of God and become mature, attaining to the whole measure of the fullness of Christ."

Psalm 68 is one of the great ascension psalms. There is a series of psalms (Psalms 120-134) all about the ascension of Jesus Christ, prophesied by David, Solomon and other psalmists. These psalms are all about looking up to the ascended LORD Jesus in heaven, looking to Him for all that the Church needs in the challenges of life. For example, Psalm 133 explains how the brothers live together in unity as the oil runs down from the head of the high priest onto his body, that is to say, the Church lives in unity when the Spirit flows down from Christ the Head onto His Body. Yet, Paul does not go to these ascension psalms in Ephesians 4 but instead goes back to an earlier ascension psalm that gives us a breathtaking account of God's ascension actually taking place. Paul quotes from verse 18 when the victorious Christ ascends to the heavenly sanctuary surrounded by the vast angelic armies, carrying the spoils of

the universe with Him. Yet, verse 19 is incredible. This triumphant God who has all power and wealth in His hands, with these millions of angels at His command does not wish to be served but to serve!

> "Praise be to the Lord, to God our Saviour, who daily bears our burdens" (Psalm 68:19).

In Psalm 68:24-27 Christ leads His people into His heavenly sanctuary, leading the great congregation in worship. In verse 28 He summons His strength and shows His power, yet the conclusion of the psalm is that all this power and strength are given to His Church, to equip them to proclaim His power and show His majesty.

> "You are awesome, O God, in your sanctuary; the God of Israel gives power and strength to His people" (Psalm 68:35).

Note: when Paul quotes Psalm 68:18 he says that Christ the LORD '*gave* gifts *to* men' but when we turn to Psalm 68:18 it says that He '*received* gifts *from* men'. When a conqueror took the spoils of war he would distribute them among his own people. Two of the oldest translations of the Hebrew understand the Hebrew in exactly the way that Paul puts it.[10] Perhaps the best way to translate the verse is "you received gifts *for* men".

The fact that the LORD God ascended back up to heaven presupposes that this LORD God had first *descended* down to the earth – verse 9. Jesus was the same LORD God of Israel who had lived in the highest heaven and dealt with His people from the beginning of the world. He came down to earth so that He could take command of the whole universe, winning His victory over all His enemies by His birth, life, death, resurrection and ascension.

10 Commenting on Psalm 68, the Rev Dr John Gill writes "*Thou hast ascended on high* – Which is to be understood, not of Moses ascending up to the firmament, as the Targum and Jarchi interpret it, of which we nowhere read; nor of David's going up to the high fortresses, as Aben Ezra; nor of God's ascent from Mount Sinai; but of Christ's ascension to heaven, as the apostle cites and explains it in (Ephesians 4:8 Ephesians 4:9); which ascension respects him as man, was not figurative, as in (Genesis 17:22); but real and local, from earth to heaven, and was certain and visible; he was seen to go up by angels and men; and, because of the certainty of it, it is here expressed in the past tense, though it was then future... *thou hast received gifts for men* – the gifts of the Holy Spirit, qualifying men for the ministry of the Gospel, as they are interpreted by the Apostle, (Ephesians 4:11); these Christ received from his divine Father in human nature, when he ascended up to heaven, in order to give them to men; and which he did in a very extraordinary manner on the day of Pentecost. The Targum and Syriac version render it, "thou hast given gifts to men"; and the Arabic version, "and he gave gifts to men", as the apostle, (Ephesians 4:8)."

Jesus uses His authority to equip the Church so that we may be built up to maturity, becoming more and more like Christ. With the whole universe at His disposal Christ's only concern is that we have everything we need to live as the Church. The purpose of the universe itself was to form the Bride of Christ into the fullness of God so that we might be married to Christ in the renewed universe forevermore. Given the significance of the Church in chapter 1 of Ephesians, this does not take us by surprise. Of course, in 1 Corinthians 12-14 Paul gives a lot more detail about how, by the Spirit, Christ equips His Church.

Paul shows how the LORD Jesus gives leaders to the Church family so that the whole family can be taught and equipped for these "works of service" that are the fullness of God. The apostles, prophets, evangelists, pastors and teachers are not given so that they alone do all these works but so that the whole family is equipped for the works of service. All these leadership roles within the Church are given to serve the Church family. We meet together to be taught, discipled and equipped so that we can go out and do the works of service that God has prepared for us throughout the whole week in our neighbourhoods, workplaces, colleges and rest homes. As we serve one another in love, so the Body of Christ is built up into that loving unity and we begin to grasp that knowledge of Jesus Christ that transcends all knowledge.

How vital these words of the apostle Paul are! What is the key to the health of our local Church? *We serve one another in love*. This is what produces unity and what takes us deeper into the true knowledge of Christ. The mark of maturity is not in how much we 'know' or how many people visit our building or what doctrinal document we stick on the wall. If we are going to attain to "the whole measure of the fullness of Christ' then we need the strength and gifts of the Spirit in order to genuinely, practically, sincerely serve one another in love and humility. That is the life and glory of the Living God.

Verse 14 is a serious warning. The pastors, teachers and evangelists must train us in the works of service (verse 12) so that we become deeply rooted and founded in the love and knowledge of Jesus. Only in this way can we have the roots and foundations that will keep us securely anchored when the false teaching and opposition comes. Unless we are listening to the Word of God taught by our Church leaders and putting the Way and Truth of Jesus into practice we are going to be vulnerable to all the different fads and fancies that float around. We will be thrown in one direction as the next 'sensational bestseller' gives one idea then thrown in another direction when the next 'shocking documentary' wheels out yet another 'new interpretation' of Jesus.

The defence against all this is to "speak the truth in love" (verse 15). Notice that neither love nor truth is enough on its own. The Pharisees had so much doctrinal truth and had a great passion for the Scriptures, but they did not have that love for Christ and therefore no real love for other people. On the other hand we have seen all kinds of modern movements that claim to be based purely on love, yet they end up in corruption and chaos because that love is not the holy and self-sacrificial love of Jesus.

The first step must always be our connection to Jesus Christ. The Man Christ Jesus is the Head of the Body: He is the source of that new humanity that defines us. We know His truth and His love because we are connected to Him. If the Church ever becomes disconnected from Jesus then it is like a body left on the guillotine after the blade falls. There can be no life or growth in a body if it is separated from its head!

Christ is the Head of the Body – and from the Head comes everything that the Body requires. Verse 16 – "From him the whole body, joined and held together by every supporting ligament, grows and builds itself up in love, as each part does its work." We do not receive gifts of the Spirit for our own personal enjoyment, so that we can have a great private spiritual life. No, the gifts that Christ gives by His Spirit operate properly only as each part does its work.

We must always be thinking how we can use our abilities to serve others. The extent to which we do this is the mark of our maturity, our growth into the likeness of Christ.

Study 4 Bible Questions
Ephesians 4:1-13

1. Verse 1 – If we look back at the end of chapter 3, what is the high calling that should shape the way we live?
2. Verse 2 – When the Father can do immeasurably more than we can ask or imagine, how can the instructions of verse 2 live up to such great power? Is this really the most that Paul can imagine?
3. Verse 3 – Why does Paul say 'make every effort' to keep united in the Spirit? How much effort do we normally put into this? Are there ever times when all our efforts are not enough to keep the unity of the Spirit?
4. Verses 4-6 – Consider all the items that Paul lists that are 'one'. Can we think of one consequence of each that should hold us all together? For example, if we all have the same baptism then we are all joined together as members of the same community, separated from the world.
5. Verse 7 – The friendship of Jesus has been given to each one of us – but this friendship gives us abilities and responsibilities. Why does Paul insist that this empowering friendship of Jesus is given to "each one of us"?
6. Verse 8 – The Hebrew of Psalm 68:18 perhaps should be translated as "He received gifts for men", but Paul brings out the relevant meaning here by quoting it as "gave gifts to men". How does Psalm 68:17-20 fill out our understanding of the ascension of Jesus?
7. Verse 9 – Psalm 68 verse 18 and verse 24 can sound strange at first. Why is the LORD God ascending? Why does he need to go back into heaven? How do Paul's comments in Ephesians 4:9 help us understand what is happening in Psalm 68?
8. Verse 10 – When we read the gospels we are sometimes shown how Jesus was tired, hungry, thirsty or sad, yet there are other times we see Him walking on water, commanding the weather, talking to Moses and Elijah who had been dead for hundreds of years, raising the dead and forgiving sins. When He was walking on earth, Jesus was also sustaining the entire universe. Why is it so important to

remember that the same Man who was crucified now fills the whole universe? How does this connect to the vast vision of the love and knowledge of Jesus at the end of chapter 3?

9. Verse 11 – Why does Jesus use the vast resources of the entire universe to provide leadership and good teaching in the local churches? Aren't there more important ways to use such cosmic power?
10. Verse 12 – What is the main responsibility of the preachers, evangelists, pastors and teachers? How much time should an evangelist spend with not-yet-Christians and how much time training the Christians?
11. Verse 13 – Given the truly incredible and breath-taking view of Jesus that Paul sets before us here, how does this motivate us to push onto maturity, unity and knowledge of Jesus?

Study 4 Further Questions

1. Various New Age philosophies, derived from Hindu religion, talk about "having the divine life within us" or even that each of us is a god. How might Paul address these claims on the basis of His prayer at the end of Ephesians chapter 3? How can human beings really be filled with the divine life?
2. If our local Church is fractured by divisions, what would be the best course of action based on our last study? What examples of serving together might produce the unity that Paul describes?
3. Ephesians 4:10 tells us that Jesus Christ fills the whole universe. One of the great debates of Church history is about the meaning of this. One group says that as a human being Jesus cannot be in more than one place at once, so Christ fills the universe in His divine nature alone. The Reformer John Calvin best represents this first view: "For even if the Word in His immeasurable essence united with the nature of man into one person, *we do not imagine that He was confined therein*. Here is something marvellous: the Son of God descended from heaven in such a way that, without leaving heaven, He willed to be borne in the virgin's womb, to go about earth, and

to hang upon the cross; yet He continuously filled the world even as He had done from the beginning." (Institutes II.13.4). The other group says that Christ is both divine and human in all places at once; that His natures cannot be divided in any way. They fear that it is dangerous to suggest that God the Word is more than Jesus of Nazareth. The Lutheran Formula of Concord states this view in Section 8, 27 – "Christ has ascended, not merely as any other saint, to heaven, but, as the apostle testifies (Eph. 4:10), above all heavens, and also truly fills all things, and *being everywhere present, not only as God, but also as man* and rules from sea to sea and to the ends of the earth; as the prophets predict, Ps. 8:1,6; 93:1f ; Zech. 9:10". So, if we consider the way that God the Son upheld the universe in 100BC, was it any different in 20AD or again in 100AD?

Study 4	**Daily Readings**
Day 1	Ephesians 3:14-21
Day 2	Ephesians 4:1-6
Day 3	Ephesians 4:7-13
Day 4	Psalm 68:1-10
Day 5	Psalm 68:11-23
Day 6	Psalm 68:24-35
Day 7	Psalm 123:1-4

The daily Bible readings are an opportunity not only to read through all of the material in the book under study, but also to read parts of the Bible that relate to the themes and issues that we have been considering. Wetry to make sure that we receive light from the whole Bible as we think through the key issues each week.

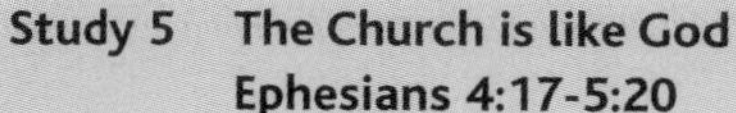

Study 5 The Church is like God
Ephesians 4:17-5:20

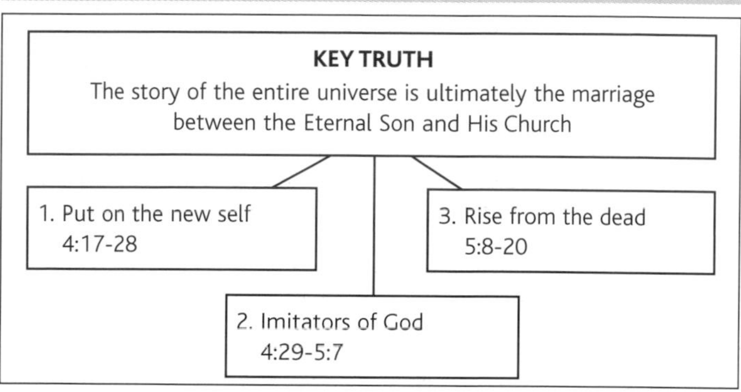

1. Put on the new self – 4:17-28

Living in the shadow of the pagan temple the Ephesians were constantly tempted to fall back into the thinking that they used to know. The life of Ephesus was based on that old way of thinking, the way of thinking that was without God and separated from Christ, without hope and enslaved to selfish desires. The old patterns of life and thought were still there, calling to the Ephesian Christians. How could they resist that call? How could they protect their thinking from "every wind of teaching" or the constant drip of the old habits of thought?

Paul is very serious in his command to them in verse 17. He does not merely 'tell' them but must 'insist on it in the LORD'. He is not offering helpful advice but issuing a stern command – "you must no longer..."

This is vital to grasp. Our confusion, depression, ignorance, feelings of alienation from God, loss of genuine feeling and enslavement to selfish desires all come when we fail to obey this command. We tend to simply allow our thoughts to 'happen', to take whatever direction they will, to follow the winds and tides of the day and the environment. Look carefully at the chain of symptoms that Paul lists in 4:17-19. Rev. Steve Levy from Swansea was very helpful in applying and explaining these truths when I needed to challenge my own futile thinking.

Futile thinking – The source of the downward cycle is returning to the old ways of thought that define the non-Christian or pagan life. These thoughts may be full of worry about what might happen or they might be picking away at doubts or listening to the attacks and false ideas of the world. When we give mental space to these things we are falling into sin and this sin will certainly produce a terrible harvest.

Darkened understanding – We will no longer understand what is happening in life. Things will no longer make sense. The very truths that once illumined us will seem confusing or even false. Our lives will seem confusing and out of control.

Separated from the life of God – We will no longer feel the reality of the Living God. We might even doubt His very existence or perhaps feel that He is no longer interested in us.

Ignorance – From being people who were supposed to grow into a vast knowledge of the Cosmic Word, the Eternal Christ who holds the entire universe together, we become shrunken shadows who no longer know even the most basic aspects of truth. We might still go through the motions for a while, but the light of knowledge has faded away.

Hardening of hearts – The fullness of God produces hearts that are soft and living, moved with love and compassion for the needs around us, but the domino effect of the futile thinking causes our hearts to become deadened. Far from serving the needs of others, we become focussed in on our own problems, fears, needs and desires.

Loss of sensitivity – As our hearts become hard so our capacity for feeling dies away too. We might turn to all kinds of experiences or stimulus in order to 'feel something', to feel 'alive'.

Indulge in every kind of impurity – Yet, the things we turn to for 'feeling', whether substances, relationships, pornography, money, leisure activities, career success, social status or anything else, will never satisfy our hunger. If we were made to grow into the very fullness of the Living God going up into a knowledge that surpasses knowledge, involved in an adventure with Christ that is beyond imagination... then all the sordid and worthless things we go after can never satisfy us and there is simply *a continual lust for more*.

This depressive whirlpool can only be broken when we address the futile thinking that lies at the start of it all. We were brought from death to life, from darkness to light, from hopelessness to glorious hope when the truth of Jesus cut right into our futile thinking and showed us the truth in Jesus.

Our thinking was radically interrupted and turned upside down by Jesus and so we must continue to conform our thoughts to Jesus every single day. We did not come to know Jesus by going along with our own futile thinking (verse 20)! We did not invent Jesus Christ from our own imaginations. The NIV translation translates verse 21 as "Surely you heard of Him..." but the Greek should really be translated as "Surely you heard Him". Jesus Himself spoke to us, in all our ignorance, unbelief and confusion. He spoke the truth to us, contradicting the lies we believed. Furthermore, as we begin to follow Him in our local Church we were taught the truth according to Jesus (verse 21b). The teachers in our Church confronted the lies and told us the truth. We must continue to confront the old patterns of futile thinking day by day.

Psalm 5 shows us the constant morning meditation of Christ: He lays His concerns before His Father (verses 1-3) and then carefully reminds Himself of the truth about the world and the wicked (verses 4-8). He declares how wrong and untrustworthy are the words of the wicked and how they must be banished for their rebellion (verses 9-10), yet the Righteous One, with all His people, find refuge, joy and favour in the LORD God.

This pattern of daily getting the truth fixed in our hearts and minds is vital. This is why the Bible has so much to say about our daily prayers, our daily Bible study, and our returning to the Living God for daily bread. When our minds fall down into that futile thinking of the pagan world we must challenge our own thinking: 'Why are you downcast, O my soul?" (Psalm 43:5).

Martin Lloyd-Jones in his helpful book on spiritual depression explains this at length:

> Have you realized that most of your unhappiness in life is due to the fact that you are *listening* to yourself instead of *talking* to yourself? Take those thoughts that come to you the moment you wake up in the morning. You have not originated them, but they start talking to you, they bring back the problems of yesterday, etc.
>
> Somebody is talking. Who is talking? Your self is talking to you. Now this man's treatment was this; instead of allowing this self to talk to him, he starts talking to himself. 'Why art thou cast down, O my soul?' he asks. His soul had been depressing him, crushing him. So he stands up and says: 'Self, listen for a moment, I will speak to you.'...
>
> The main art in the matter of spiritual living is to know how to handle yourself. You have to take yourself in hand, you have to address yourself, preach to yourself, question yourself. You must say to your soul: 'Why art thou cast down'– what business have you to be disquieted?
>
> You must turn on yourself, upbraid yourself, condemn yourself, exhort yourself, and say to yourself: 'Hope thou in God'– instead of muttering in this depressed, unhappy way. And then you must go on to remind yourself of God, Who God is, and what God is and what God has done, and what God has pledged Himself to do.
>
> Then having done that, end on this great note: defy yourself, and defy other people, and defy the devil and the whole world, and say with this man: 'I shall yet praise Him for the help of His countenance, who is also the health of my countenance and my God.'[11]

Verses 22-4 give the comprehensive remedy. Instead of falling back into the old humanity with its futile thinking, we must have a new attitude in our minds, putting on the new humanity which was created for that fullness of God of 3:19 and 4:13.

11 Martyn Lloyd-Jones, *Spiritual Depression: Its Causes and Its Cure* (Grand Rapids: Eerdmans, 2002), 20-1.

> You were taught, with regard to your former way of life, to put off your old self, which is being corrupted by its deceitful desires; to be made new in the attitude of your minds; and to put on the new self, created to be like God in true righteousness and holiness.

As regards that old way of life, that old humanity, the non-Christian patterns that still surround us, we must consciously and deliberately take it off and reject it. Yet, we cannot simply 'put off' the old without replacing it with the new. Jesus has given us His new humanity, but this new life plants its flag in 'the attitude of your minds'. The Greek word for 'repentance' literally means 'a new mind' and this is precisely what we need to consciously grasp as we awake each morning. If we are going to put on the new self and get rid of the old, then we need to conform our minds to the mind of Christ: we need to learn His truth, memorise His teaching, meditate on His works.

If we are going to live that life of God, if we are really going to live like God Himself serving others in unity and love, then we cannot allow those old patterns of thought to fester away. If we are going to live "in true righteousness and holiness" then we need to take responsibility for the way we think.

So, to get down to the practical specifics, Paul begins by examining the way we deal with the truth. If our minds are going to be daily rooted in truth and produce lives of love, then our commitment to telling the truth needs to be absolute.

I was speaking to someone from the North Africa this last week who was telling me of the power that verbal contracts still have in his home. Some Bedouin traders will not sign any contract at all because to even ask them to sign a written contract is implying that you don't trust their word. Such an attitude to truth telling seems almost unimaginable for most of the modern world. Verbal contracts don't seem to be worth the paper they are written on and all our agreements need to be signed, counter-signed and guarded with endless small print because we are so fundamentally alienated from God in our general culture.

Yet, in the Church of Living God we are to be counter-revolutionaries in the Name of Jesus, the One who is the Truth. We put off the old way of falsehood (verse 25) and instead speak in plain and open truth with everyone in the Church family (and to everyone else, of course!).

The Christian Church is formed by truth telling – therefore our lifestyle with each other must be one of truth telling. There can be nothing so incongruous as Christians telling lies to each other. How are we to be a light to the world, how can the world ever realize that the truth has been spoken if we are not outstanding in our truthfulness?

Verses 26-28. Every aspect of our lives must bear this same mark of integrity. The devil wants to get a foothold by discrediting our lifestyles. Our words, even *though* they are the words of truth, will sound empty and hollow if we are noted for fits of temper and stealing. The devil cannot stand against the Word of God, but he can encourage the messengers of the Word of God to so undermine the Word of God that it is never heard for what it is. If we are seen to speak and act falsely, then even when we speak the truth, it will not ring true.

We dare not go to bed if we are angry with a brother or sister. Psalm 4:4 reminds us that as we can only find real rest when the light of Christ's face is shining upon us. If we are harbouring angry or bitter thoughts we need to search our hearts and put that anger away (Psalm 4:4), offering to the LORD that fragrant offering of self-sacrificial love as we trust in Christ alone (Psalm 4:5).

Notice how we not only put off the old self but always put on the new one. The thief must no longer steal but he must also work to produce what is useful. If he used to take things from people now he must get things to share with those in need (4:28).

So, verse 29, "do not let any unwholesome talk come out of your mouths, but only what is helpful for building others up according to their needs, that it may benefit those who listen."

Yet, our words should always be helpful for building up others according to their needs. This doesn't mean that we only ever say nice things to each other, because *often* what I need to build me up is for a fellow Christian to love me enough to show me where I am going wrong.

But, we all need words of encouragement and comfort too. The simple principle that the Bible gives us here is this – *will my words be of benefit to those who hear them?*

Well, does it really matter? Surely mere words can't matter so much? Verse 30 – integrity in our speech matters so much that when we fail we actually grieve the Holy Spirit.

This verse is a deeply moving verse. The Holy Spirit has been given to us as a seal, a deposit, until the day of redemption. He cannot leave us. God has guaranteed us a part in the new creation and this guarantee is backed up with a deposit – the Holy Spirit.

We know that we lose a deposit if we do not fulfil our purchase so, God loses His Holy Spirit if we are not kept safely till the day of redemption.

This tells us that one thing is more certain than life itself – the Holy Spirit is not going to leave us at any time in the Christian life. Like it or not, He is stuck with us for the duration.

This is why we must rid ourselves of all unwholesome speech, bitterness, rage and anger, brawling and slander, along with every form of malice (verse 31). The Holy Spirit cannot simply leave us while we indulge these evils. He lives within us and must suffer the presence of such uncleanness right before His face.

2. Imitators of God 4:29-5:7

The Holy Spirit has enjoyed the holy, gentle, pure loving company of the Father and the Son for everlasting ages, and now He finds Himself loving and redeeming Christians who force Him to witness wickedness at first hand.

No wonder He is grieved! Grief is such a deep emotion. It is about having one's heart broken, about deep pain. The Spirit longs for that fullness of the life of God, that life of unity and love. So, instead of falling back into the old patterns of life and thought we are to make the Holy Spirit feel more at home. Verse 32 and 5:1 – "Be kind and compassionate to one another, forgiving each other, just as in Christ God forgave you. Be imitators of God, therefore, as dearly loved children."

Only if we imitate God will the Holy Spirit not be grieved. Only as we live as the children of God do we respect His presence with us.

We *must* live out the gospel that is our life and hope. We can be kind and compassionate to each other, unconcerned about getting paid back, because we have been shown the greatness possible kindness and compassion and forgiveness by the Father in Jesus Christ.

We can speak honestly to each other, because we no longer have anything to hide. We have faced up to the truth about what we are outside of Christ. We know that naturally we are all addicted to "every kind of impurity, with a continual lust for more", and we know that no amount of self-righteousness impresses God. Therefore we are free to be honest with each other, forgiving when we sin against each other. We can speak the truth, because we have nothing to fear from the truth. Only the Christian knows what it is to stand under the all-seeing eyes of the terribly Holy God – and yet, we have found grace and forgiveness and cleansing and life.

The life of God is a life of love (5:1-2). Christ showed us that fullness of the life of God when He loved us and "gave Himself up for us". That self-sacrifice for others produced a fragrant offering, a fragrance that pleased the Living God. Throughout the books of Leviticus and Numbers we read how certain offerings were fragrant to the LORD (Lev 1:9, 13, 17; 2:2, 9; 3:5; 4:31; 6:15, 21; 17:6; 23:18; Num 15:3, 7, 10, 13-14, 24; 18:17; 28:2, 8, 24, 27; 29:2, 8, 13, 36). These offerings were all signs pointing to that perfect self-offering of God the Son Himself, the offering that shows us what the life and love of God looks like.

So, among us who are the dearly loved children of the Heavenly Father, we are to reject everything from that old life of futile thinking and selfish desires. We cannot touch those old ways without being defiled by them. Even the slightest hint of sexual immorality needs to be strongly resisted, as too with all impurity and greed. The moment we tolerate any of these things within the local Church we are grieving the Holy Spirit. He is called the 'Holy' Spirit because He is so absolutely dedicated to the life of God. He cannot live at peace even the slightest hint of sin. As God's holy people we must share His dedication (verse 3).

This dedication needs constant care and attention. It is so easy to relax our guard and fall into what we think of as 'harmless fun' as we share "foolish talk or coarse joking" (verse 4). We might imagine that these things 'show that we are human' but in reality they dehumanise us and take us back into the alienated and futile ways of the old self. Paul reminds us of the stark truth: there is no possibility of any of these things having a place in the kingdom of God, in the courts of heaven or the new creation future. If we want to hold onto our greed, coarse jokes, impurity and foolish talk then there can be no place for us either (verse 5). There will always be those who tell us to relax and to 'loosen up' because these things are not to be taken so seriously. However, these are empty, dangerous words full of deception. The truth is that the Living God is filled with wrath about impurity and greed: His judgment will certainly fall on those who hold to these sins.

Verse 7 brings the matter home to us: not only must we root these things out in our own lives but we cannot share our lives with those who take a careless view of them. Here Paul is probably thinking of those who claim the name of Christ and yet carry on with those old futile ways. They are poisonous because they will drag us down into their confusion and judgment.

3. Rise from the dead – 5:8-20

Paul now draws together what he has been teaching since 4:17. Everyone in the local Church was once going along with the ways of the world, the flesh and the devil (as Paul so thoroughly showed back in 2:1-3). The fact that we trusted in Christ when we heard of Him is not the end of the story. We are called on and up into the love and knowledge of the fullness of God in Christ. This happens as we daily repent: we daily change our mind and reject the old futile way of thinking and deliberately, consciously put on that new attitude of mind shaped by the truth according to Jesus. From this new mind we live out the life of self-sacrificial love as we forgive and serve one another in the unity of the Spirit. This obedience to the Way of Jesus means that we will experience His presence dwelling in our hearts and we will come to know that ever-expanding horizon of the love of Jesus.

Once we were darkness, but now we are light in the Lord Jesus (5:8). The contrast between the old life/mind and the new could not be expressed in sharper terms. If this is what we are then our lives must be filled with the light of goodness and truth (5:9). If our old obsessions were about finding out how to please ourselves, now, as we grow into the knowledge of the Son of God (4:13) we are obsessed with finding out what pleases *Him* (verse 10).

In verses 11-14 Paul seems to be saying that as our lives become filled with the light of goodness and truth so the fruitless deeds of darkness are exposed by the light. The more the light shines in our Church family so it is harder for the darkness to exist. Evil likes to hide in the darkness and keep everything secret 5:12. Masks, mobs and anonymity are the allies of evil because they provide a cover for dark deeds. By contrast, the family of God lives in the light, confessing their sins to one another and living in truth, love and goodness.

Verse 14 seems to introduce either a quotation from the Scriptures or at least a summary of some of the Scriptures. It is just possible that Paul might be quoting a popular Christian hymn of the time, but this formula is normally used to introduce Scripture. There are several parts of Isaiah's prophecy that Paul seems to have in mind here.

> Isaiah 9:2 – "The people walking in darkness have seen a great light; on those living in the land of the shadow of death a light has dawned."
>
> Isaiah 59:8 and 60:1-2 – "We look for light, but all is darkness; for brightness, but we walk in deep shadows... Arise, shine, for your light has come, and the glory of the LORD rises upon you. See, darkness covers the earth and thick darkness is over the peoples, but the LORD rises upon you and his glory appears over you."

From the darkness and death of the old and futile ways, we turn to Christ who shines His light on us. So we need to be very careful how we live (verse 15). If we live carelessly and unwisely we will waste our lives in the depression, futility and darkness that we used to be enslaved to.

As in Genesis chapter 1, the light brings life and 'fruit', whereas the darkness is 'fruitless'. Darkness is nothing at all: it is the mere absence of light. The deeds of the darkness produce nothing that will last, nothing of value.

The days are evil (verse 16) seems to mean that the earth is filled with thick darkness and naturally our time will be used in the futile and worthless pursuit of our evil desires. Rather we "make the most of every opportunity" or more literally we "buy back the time", redeeming it from the futility of the darkness. As we use our time in living the life of God so these fleeting hours that we have can be invested in eternal treasure.

> Jonathan Edwards, the philosopher-theologian who became God's instrument in the 'Great Awakening' in America in 1734–5, wrote in the seventieth of his famous Resolutions just before his twentieth birthday: 'Resolved: Never to lose one moment of time, but to improve it in the most profitable way I possibly can.' He was a wise man, for the first sign of wisdom which Paul gives here is a disciplined use of time.[12]

If we are going to use our time well and invest for eternity with fruit to show on that final day, then of course we do not look for our 'highs' through alcohol or drugs (verse 18). The Bible is filled with this same wisdom – Proverbs 20:1; 23:19-21, 26-35; Hosea 4:11. The key issue here is keeping a clear and responsible mind. If the battle is for our mind and our thinking then anything that weakens our thinking is to be avoided at all costs.

Instead we find our 'high' in the Spirit of the Living God, rejoicing in Him. People might say that it is miserable to avoid drunkenness, but in fact we are to fill our meeting times with the singing and music. In fact, each one of us is to "sing and make music" in our hearts to the LORD (verses 19-20). Music is such a distinctive feature of the Church family and down through history music and songs have poured out of the Church. Every generation of the saints produces new songs and new music, often innovating new musical forms in the joy of the Spirit. When people first join a Church family they may never have experienced singing together in the way that is so common in all local churches.

12 Stott, J. R. W. (1979). *God's new society: The message of Ephesians* (202). Downers Grove, Ill.: InterVarsity Press.

The key to this joyful and exuberant attitude to life is gratitude. Verse 20 reminds us to be grateful about everything, all the time. The grumbling heart has become alienated from the Father and looks for what is wrong, but the wise and mature heart gives thanks to the Father in the name of Jesus in every situation. There are always many things to be thankful for and the heart that is filled with the Spirit finds opportunities for giving thanks throughout each day.

Study 5 Bible Questions

Ephesians 4:29-5:7

1. Verse 29 – If we are to avoid 'rotten' speech, what are the three essential features that Paul sets out for all of our speech?
2. Verse 30 – Why does Paul suddenly warn us about grieving the Holy Spirit in the middle of these commands? What does this tell us about what grieves the Spirit?
3. Verse 31-32 – How does the example of God in Christ stand as the opposite of all the things listed in verse 32?
4. Chapter 5, verse 1-2 – Satan originally tempted us to be like God, but his way of doing that led to the murder of the whole human race. What is the true way to imitate the Living God? Why does Paul tell us to be like God "as dearly loved children"?
5. Verse 3 – Why is Paul so very careful about even a 'hint' of sexual immorality? Why is this such a powerful desire, in the light of verses 1-2?
6. Verse 4 – What kind of good speech is the cure for all the bad speech? Why is that? What kind of attitude does each produce?
7. Verse 5 – How can anybody be saved if this verse is true? These sins are found in all of us, so can any of us ever enter the kingdom of Christ?
8. Verses 6-7 – There are always people who say that God will not really judge the world, that in the end He will overlook all these sins. How should we deal with such people? Does it make a difference whether these people claim to be Christians or not?
9. If our goal as a local Church is to live the life of the Living God, then what practical changes can we make in the coming weeks to guide us nearer to that?

Study 5 Further Questions

1. Depression is one of the most common problems in modern life. It is said that up to 1 in 7 people will go through this. How does Paul's cycle of futile thinking compare to the experience of depression? What would be the impact for a depressed person if they went for a 20-minute walk each day with some important Bible truths to learn? In depression the futile thinking seems to take over, but what are the best ways to counter that futile thinking with the truth in Jesus?
2. If our basic battle each day is for the attitude of our mind, then what is the relevance of the things we read, the television we watch, the music we listen to and the images we see? How much time do we spend each day taking in the truth according to Jesus and how much time do we absorb the truth according to advertising companies, the entertainment industry, the news agencies, the chat shows, the sports world etc?

Study 5 Daily Readings

Day 1	Ephesians 4:17-28
Day 2	Ephesians 4:29-5:7
Day 3	Ephesians 5:8-20
Day 4	Luke 6:27-36
Day 5	Luke 6:37-49
Day 6	2 Peter 1:3-11
Day 7	James 3:1-12

The daily Bible readings are an opportunity not only to read through all of the material in the book under study, but also to read parts of the Bible that relate to the themes and issues that we have been considering. Wetry to make sure that we receive light from the whole Bible as we think through the key issues each week.

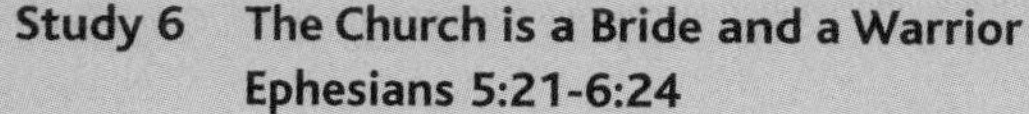

Study 6 The Church is a Bride and a Warrior
Ephesians 5:21-6:24

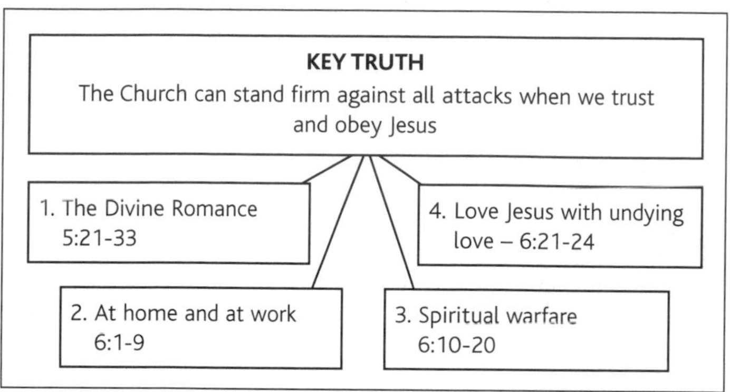

1. The Divine Romance – 5:21-33

The Ephesians were to be shining light displaying the fullness of God right in the heart of a city dominated by a massive pagan temple. The old patterns of life and thinking were always around them, but the truth and love of Jesus are always so much more than those futile ways of darkness.

In every age, in every place, the clear sign of the life of God is self-sacrificial love that puts the interests of others ahead of our own. So, as Paul comes to the conclusion of the letter he addresses all the different areas of our day-to-day life to show what the way of Jesus looks like.

He begins with the foundational revolution: we submit to each other, in all situations, out of reverence for Christ. This is yet another way of describing how the local Church is to be rooted and grounded in love, but the word 'submit' is always a flash point for us. Jesus submitted to His Father in all things, most famously in the Garden of Gethsemane (Matthew 26:36-46). He washed His disciples feet as He was preparing for His death (John 13:1-17). As Jesus Himself said "I have set you an example that you should do as I have done for you. Very truly I tell you, no servant is greater than his master, nor is a messenger greater than the one who sent him. Now that you know these things, you will be blessed if you do them" (John 13:15-17).

This pattern of submitting to and serving others is the constant pattern of our life together. Paul begins by applying it to marriage. It is quite possible that sexuality raised strong issues in a city dominated by the temple to Artemis, possibly with temple prostitutes and ideas about marriage in general.

Here we come to a picture of the Church that is found throughout the whole Bible, especially in the Old Testament. *The Church is the Bride of Christ.*

When we were brought into the Church by the gospel it wasn't just some legal transaction. We were being brought into a romance, a cosmic spiritual love affair. The greatest glory of the Church is that we are betrothed to Christ, the Eternal Son of God. This is the ultimate example of marrying above our social status! The Church is heading towards its wedding day, when the Bridegroom will come to prepare the family home for an everlasting marriage. As in certain Asian weddings, it is the Bride who is longing for the arrival of the Bridegroom.

Nothing is too much trouble to Christ for His Bride. So much so that He even dies for her. He came to serve and not to be served. His sole concern is for the good of the Church, that she might be utterly radiant, free from everything that might spoil her. Christ uses all His resources for the good of the Church.

Mixing metaphors a little Paul explains that Christ cares for the Church with just the same care that a person has for their own body. The instinct to get away from pain and avoid harm is basic to us all. Christ has that same instinct for the Church, preserving her from anything that would damage her. Christ does not abandon this betrothal because He doesn't feel fulfilled in the relationship anymore. No, He makes no distinction between His own good and that of the Church.

When quoting Genesis 2:24 in 5:31 Paul indicates that these foundational verses about Adam and Eve were also about Christ and the Church. Yes, we are taken into a 'profound mystery' here as we learn that the Eternal Son of God becomes one flesh with His Church.

This truth about the Church should never be far from our hearts and minds. Salvation is a romance – it's about love between Christ and His

Church. We can never fall into legalism or formalism once we are caught up into this reality. The Bible is a love letter not an authoritarian set of commands like 'religious texts'. Remember that Paul's prayer was that the Ephesian Church would grasp the multi-dimensional love of Christ that surpasses knowledge, and through that to enter into the fullness of God!

With this glorious romance in our minds, Paul shows us how we can try to mirror this in our own marriages in this life. Yes, the Church is served by Christ in amazing ways, yet she also trusts Him and accepts His leadership and guidance. Within the Trinity the Son always submits to the will of the Father and yet He is fully God in just the same way that the Father is fully God. In the life of God there is not even a hint that submission implies that the Son is less divine than the Father![13] So the wife's submission to her husband for the sake of Christ must never have any hint of subservience or inequality. As the wife honours her husband by putting her trust in him and accepting his leadership of the marriage and family, so she shows how the Church relates to Christ, but also how the Son relates to the Father (see 1 Corinthians 11:3).

If the husband's job is to follow Christ's pattern of self-sacrificial service for the Church, then it is vital that his wife accepts this service and supports his efforts to meet this high standard.

I have met Christian men who are always going on about Ephesians 5:22 – but in truth Paul is not even talking to them! When Paul addresses husbands from verse 25 we have more than enough to worry about. In the darkness men may try to dominate and use women, but in the light we can show what the life of God looks like in a marriage. It is our job to do whatever it takes, even to the cost of our own lives, to build up and support our wives.

In marriage all this has so many applications. If Christ is so determined to protect the Church from impurity, preserving her as holy and blameless, then what does this mean for the way a husband treats his wife and relates to her in the most intimate of ways? The wife who puts down or criticises her husband in front of others is doing great harm to their marriage and to the way that others will think of Christ and the Church.

13 It is interesting how the cults who deny the divinity of the Son try to deal with this teaching (and especially 1 Corinthians 11:3) because the clear implication would be that women are not as human as men!

Christ and the Church form one whole Body (5:29) with a complete sharing of life and possessions. This too means that there must be a transparency and complete sharing of life, possessions, money and plans within a marriage. When Paul quotes Genesis 2:24 in verse 31 we are reminded of how the husband's union with his wife must take priority over his old family relationship. However much he may have been pampered by his mother, the number one woman in his life must always be his wife!

Paul summarises all this with verse 33 – "Each one of you also must love his wife as he loves himself, and the wife must respect her husband." Many have pointed out that Paul seems to put a heavier burden on the husbands than on the wives, but we should not read too much into that.

2. At home and at work – 6:1-9

> God is calling on us to be different from the world. We're to have different marriages, different families, and different life-styles. In Ephesians, Paul says we're not to walk as the heathen walk (4:17). We're to walk in love (5:2), not in lust; in light (5:8), not in darkness; in wisdom (5:15), not in foolishness; in the Spirit (5:18), not in the flesh. We're not to be selfish—each man for himself; we're to be unselfish—each for the other. We're not to be possessed by our own ego; we're to be controlled by the Spirit of God. We're to be different.[14]

Right from Genesis 17 the LORD God has commanded his people to disciple their children in the Way of Jesus within the Church. Children will always be self-willed and need to be disciplined, yet Paul is not only interested in the general obedience of parents to children. Their obedience is to be 'in the Lord', just as the wife was to submit and the husband to serve for Christ. Always Christ Jesus must be at the centre of family life. When we ask one another how our children are doing, what do we say? All too often our first reply is to do with education or sport rather than their faithfulness and maturity in Christ. In fact, there are even examples of parents putting a higher priority on educational success than Christian growth and development!

14 MacArthur, J. (1997). *The Fulfilled Family*. Chicago: Moody Press. Chapter 8, introduction.

Paul refers us back to the fifth commandment, as recorded in Deuteronomy 5:16. Deuteronomy 6:4-9 and 20-25 describe how godly parents were to teach their children the way of the LORD, bringing them up as disciples of the Promised Messiah. So, the fifth commandment needs to be understood in that context: "Honour your father and mother, as the LORD your God has commanded you, so that you may live long and that it may go well with you in the land the LORD your God is giving you."

Notice how Paul brings out the real intention of Moses when he says "...that it may go well with you and that you may enjoy long life *on the earth."* The ancient promises about inheriting the land of Canaan were pointing to that glorious new creation future when the whole earth will be the home of righteousness. This is what Abraham himself understood when he was called to go to the land of Canaan at the very beginning – see Hebrews 11:8-10.

So, the fifth commandment is not simply promising that obedient children will live to be 80 years of age but something far more important than that. If the parents are teaching their children the way of Jesus and the children listen to this instruction then they too will inherit the 'long life' of the resurrection in that new creation future. Just as Jesus promised that the meek will inherit the earth, so the children who obey the gospel teaching of their parents will inherit everlastingly long life on the earth!

Of course, this does throw the responsibility back onto the parents. What are we really teaching our children, not just in our words but also in the way that we live our lives? What are the truths we teach by the choices we make, the priorities we pursue, the financial commitments we make? Do our marriages show our children what Christ and the Church are like? Is the local Church the very centre of our community life or do we keep it to one side so that we can pursue a futile agenda?

Yet, on the other hand, Paul is aware that damage can be done by an over-zealous parent who expects too much from their children. Our heavenly Father deals with us with great patience and compassion, always receiving us when we come back to Him. Our training and instruction must always be according to the Way of Jesus Himself (verse 4). Look how Jesus instructed the disciples throughout the gospels. They were slow to learn and let Him down in many ways, yet He never condemned them or rejected them. Again, there are examples of parents who literally refuse to speak to their children if their children have disappointed their expectations! All of this legalism and paganism belongs to the futile ways of darkness.

From the home, now Paul turns to the workplace. Much of our lives is spent working alongside those who do not yet know Jesus, so it is vital that we know how to make the teaching of Jesus attractive in our workplace (see Titus 2:10). Paul is of course dealing with a workplace that was defined by slaves and masters rather than employers and employees, so we can be sure that whatever will work in the extreme conditions of slavery will certainly work in the less severe conditions that most of us face.

Most of his readers will have faced slavery in their workplace, so most of his instructions deal with those challenges. Just as submission was the secret to the unity and love of the local Church, marriage and the family, so it is also the secret to the workplace, even under the conditions of slavery. Our first instincts might always be to fight for our rights and assert ourselves, yet the Way of Jesus teaches us another way.

The workers who belong to Jesus are to obey their earthly masters just as if they were serving Christ Himself! (6:5). Genuine respect and honour is to be given to the bosses, with real sincerity of heart. Remember again that Paul is not speaking here of the regulated conditions of the modern workplace where the worker can resign. Paul is speaking of working conditions where cruelty and abuse was common and where the slaves had no rights at all. To show sincere respect under such conditions can only come by the power and love of Christ Himself.

Furthermore, this respect and integrity of work is to govern the worker whether the boss is around or not. Even when the work is not seen, it must be done as if Jesus Himself were asking it from us (verse 6).

The Marxist revolution called on the workers to rise up and overthrow the bosses, but the much more powerful and radical revolution of Jesus calls on His workers to serve their bosses with wholehearted integrity as if the LORD Himself were in charge. It sounds as if this is a revolution that would never change anything and yet it is the followers of Jesus who have overthrown slavery, improved working conditions and dignified labour infinitely more than all the slave revolts and rebellions of history.

The bosses or masters who belong to Jesus must also bring His revolution into the workplace. Instead of lording their authority over their slaves and workers, the Christian boss remembers that he too is a slave of the LORD Jesus (verse 9) and he must serve that Master just as his workers serve him.

In Matthew 20:25-28 Jesus explains the difference between the pagan use of authority and how it must be used with His followers.

> Jesus called them together and said, "You know that the rulers of the Gentiles lord it over them, and their high officials exercise authority over them. Not so with you. Instead, whoever wants to become great among you must be your servant, and whoever wants to be first must be your slave — just as the Son of Man did not come to be served, but to serve, and to give his life as a ransom for many."

The LORD in heaven sees no difference between the lowliest slave on earth and the highest CEO of the biggest company: He is the Master of all. Just as Paul told us to get the new attitude of mind in 4:23, so each day we need to deliberately and consciously teach ourselves that Christ Jesus is with us in our workplace or college, in our home or study. Everything that we do must be done as if we were working directly for Him.

> Our great need is the clear-sightedness to see Jesus Christ and to set him before us. It is possible for the housewife to cook a meal as if Jesus Christ were going to eat it, or to spring-clean the house as if Jesus Christ were to be the honoured guest. It is possible for teachers to educate children, for doctors to treat patients and nurses to care for them, for solicitors to help clients, shop assistants to serve customers, accountants to audit books and secretaries to type letters as if in each case they were serving Jesus Christ. Can the same be said in relation to the masses of industrial workers with tedious routine machine-minding to do, and to miners who have to work underground? Surely yes. The presence of Christ in the mine or factory is certainly no excuse for bad conditions. On the contrary, it should be a spur to improving them.[15]

15 Stott, J. R. W. (1979). *God's new society: The message of Ephesians* (252–253). Downers Grove, Ill.: InterVarsity Press.

3. Spiritual warfare – 6:10-20

The devil wants us to please ourselves. He wants us to spend our lives doing what **WE** want to do. He wants us to look after 'number one'. As long as I do what **I** please, then I am *controlled* not by myself, but by the devil.

As we come to the end of the Paul's letter to the Ephesians, the great apostle sets the Church in its cosmic context, attacked by the devil and his servants, but standing firm in the Way, Truth and Life of Jesus Christ. Everything we have learned in the previous chapters of Ephesians was the practice of spiritual warfare – in Church unity, marriage, the family, the workplace, but now we look behind the scenes. Spiritual warfare is not about directly fighting with demons but living out this love and truth of Jesus when we are surrounded by all the pressures to go back to the old ways of thinking and acting.

Here we are taken to the front line of spiritual warfare for a view from the trenches and what we learn about this war is *not* what popular culture tells us about fighting supernatural enemies. In the movies and novels, supernatural enemies are stupid, obvious, crass and ugly. They are overcome by adventurous heroes with machine-guns, swords and brute force. Paul tells us the truth. The first thing we need for spiritual warfare is a *rejection* of our own strength, an awareness of how feeble we are in such confrontations.

Verse 10. Anyone who thinks of himself as skilful or powerful in supernatural combat is a loser from the very start. They have already been beaten by the devil. We must let ourselves be strengthened in the LORD with *HIS* mighty power. That mighty power in Ephesians 1 and 2 brought Jesus back from the dead and brought us to new birth. We were powerless against the devil in chapter 2:1-3 and if we ever forget *that* we cannot stand.

Verse 11, in *HIS* strength we put on *HIS* armour. The Living God allows us to put on His own armour, the very armour that He wears when He goes out to battle. We have seen how God lives with love and unity: Jesus carried on living that light of life right through the Cross. Paul will show us how to make the same stand, living the same way, defended just as Jesus was.

We are to renounce all our own strategies and wisdom, and with the LORD's strength and armour we are to take our stand, verse 11, "against the devil's schemes". The enemy of the Church is not flesh and blood – verse 12. Our enemy is the devil and his evil spirits: the rulers, authorities, powers and forces in the 'heavenly realms'. This is more than private conflicts that we might have with individual people in our workplace or neighbourhood. The futile ways of thinking and the selfish ways of living belong to a much bigger empire of darkness that is maintained and manipulated by Satan (just as he did at the beginning in Genesis 2). Written into the structures and institutions of the world, these dark patterns of thought exercise an influence far beyond the personal conflicts that may seem to be most immediate.

The moment we see the battle in the world today as merely a battle among human beings we will have lost the agenda of Jesus Christ. We will resort to the armour and weapons of flesh and blood to fight against flesh and blood. Not just in the sense of swords and guns, but also politics, money, influence, status, power and prestige. If we invest in *such* weapons and defence, then we are no longer fighting the real battle: we have simply become casualties of the spiritual war. Yes, the structures of society may be changed by the Church of Jesus Christ, but the centre of our revolution is the local Church where the life of God is actually put into practice and shines out to the glory of God.

So, who is the real enemy and how do we fight this enemy?

Verse 11. The enemy general is the devil and he has strategic and tactical schemes for the battle. Under him he has a whole military staff and command structure: rulers, authorities, powers and spiritual forces. They are all based in the *heavenly realms*, but exert their strategy over this dark world.

First, what is their strategy? What schemes does the devil have?

This is not a mysterious subject. If we go through the Bible and see how the devil thinks, his overall philosophy is easy to see. When we see him at the beginning of the book of Job, his thinking is that people are motivated by getting what they want, getting the good things in life. When he tempts Jesus in the wilderness, his strategy is the same.

"If you are hungry, you should use your power to feed yourself. If you want people to follow you, then show off to them. If you want the world's glory, then I will give it to you." When Judas was possessed by Satan, it was because he wanted money. When Peter fell temporarily under the power of Satan in Mark 8, it was because Peter wanted Jesus to avoid the suffering and shame of the Cross. Jesus immediately recognised whose voice it was when He heard Peter telling Him just what He wanted to hear. Here in Ephesians, chapter 2:1-3, the devil encourages us to gratify our desires, to do just what we want.

He will always tell us that it is a good thing to do what we want rather than following the way of Jesus Christ. The devil's schemes are simple, but powerful. He will always offer us ease and comfort and pleasure *if* we will follow him. The choice he puts before us every day of our lives in this dark and dying world is the choice between pleasing ourselves and following Christ.

Spiritual warfare rarely involves people foaming at the mouth invoking the name of their dark lord.[16] Every day, if we are following Jesus Christ, we are in the very thick of spiritual warfare: every time we say 'no' to our evil desires and live the Way of Jesus we stand against the devil's schemes. Every time we step out of the comfort zone to show the Way and Life of Jesus to our next-door neighbours we have stood our ground in Christ. Every time we choose love and forgiveness in our lives together, we deny the devil a foothold among us – 4:27. Every time our marriages reflect Christ's sacrifice for the Church, or we take the time to train our children in the love and truth of Jesus, or we stick our necks out to tell someone about Jesus, all these occasions are times when we stand against the devil's schemes.

The devil is not trying to get us all to become spell-casting voodoo doctors. If there is too much of *that* kind of thing people might get nervous and start thinking seriously about spiritual matters. The devil is

16 There are occasions when the Church might ask the LORD Jesus to cast out demons, but notice how relatively infrequent they were in the lives of the apostles. The apostles went to cities that were dominated by dark spiritual powers, yet they did not go out to seek confrontation. They did not go around driving demons out of everyone they met. Note especially how reluctant Paul was to deal directly with the unclean spirit in Acts 16:16-18.

much more interested in us simply investing in the 'here and now' rather than the new creation. If we live as if there is no resurrection morning, as if Jesus will never return, as if this life is all we have then the devil's scheme has succeeded. Conspicuously 'evil' behaviour is nothing more than the devil's sideshow.

If we are not yet followers of Jesus Christ, we are not yet involved in this conflict. Anyone who does not believe in Jesus, according to the Bible, is under the power of the devil. As long as we believe The Lie that the devil constantly tells us, then we cannot possibly stand against him in any meaningful sense. As soon as we trust in Jesus our eyes are opened and we find ourselves on the front-line of a spiritual engagement. Once again we realise how important it is to keep our minds conformed to the truth of Jesus. If we are not consistently and regularly filling our minds with the words of Scripture we will find the devil's lies creeping in and controlling us.

At first we might be a little intimidated by these evil forces listed here in verse 12. These evil spiritual forces are described throughout the Bible, standing behind human individuals, institutions, cultures and nations. They constantly work the devil's schemes in this present darkness. None of us can defeat even one of them in our own strength. But, we must see them in the context of the whole book of Ephesians. They are based in the heavenly realms, verse 12. Now, what do we know of the heavenly realms?

> Ephesians 2:6 – "God raised us up with Christ and seated us with him in the heavenly realms in Christ Jesus..."

So, where does that place us? Is Jesus able to hold His own in the heavenly realms? Can He cope with all these evil spiritual forces? Is He threatened by them?

Ephesians 1:20-22. God the Father exercised His mighty power "in Christ when he raised him from the dead and seated him at his right hand in the heavenly realms, *far above all rule and authority, power and dominion,* and every title that can be given, not only in the present age but also in the one to come. And God placed all things under his feet and appointed him to be head over everything for the Church."

Jesus and His Church are seated *far above* these rulers, authorities and powers. These evil forces are *under His feet*. In Jesus we need not fear them. If we resist them in Jesus, through the gospel, they will run away from us, as the Bible promises in James 4:7-8.

So, this spiritual battle has already been won by Jesus... and we must never forget this. It is quite wrong for our attention to become fixed on these evil spirits as if we needed to achieve the victory ourselves. Too many Christians have become fascinated by these unseen enemies and in doing so reject the armour of God and give them far too much power.

Instead of simply calling on the Name of Jesus and focusing entirely on living out His truth and love, many get drawn into trying to name all the demons and focusing on *them*. It is important to remember that when Paul was in Ephesus there were a bunch of 'ghostbusters': seven brothers who went around trying to engage the evil spirits directly 'in the name of Jesus' – Acts 19:13-16. These seven sons of Sceva made no impact on the evil spirits; in fact they got beaten up.

Prof Max Turner wrote "[in the Bible] the apostles and others take action where people are discerned as being affected by malignant spirits (Acts 16:16-18), but there is no attempt at seek-and-destroy missions. Nor is there any word about the apostolic Church attempting to identify and bind higher level spiritual powers or territorial spirits... From the repeated exhortation to stand and withstand (6:13-14), it is clear that the battle is viewed mainly as a defensive one (not a charge into the enemy ranks). The army of the Church holds the strong high ground by virtue of its union with Christ 'far above' all the powers (1:21; 2:6): it must not allow the enemy to dislodge it from that strategic position, but repel the invader."

So, in the light of all this, what are we to do?

We are to *stand* in the armour of God – verses 13-14.

We shouldn't get too fixated upon the exact layout of this armour and weaponry, because we get different descriptions of it in Romans 13:12-14; 2 Corinthians 6:7; and 1 Thessalonians 5:8. We don't want to end up with clear mental pictures of bits of armour but very little idea of what we are supposed to do.

Rather, let's notice the key features and the main point of what Paul is saying. The armour is made up of truth, righteousness, faith and salvation. That seems a fairly simple description of the gospel itself: a list of the main features of the Way, Truth and Life of Jesus. The good news is the truth that saves us by making us righteous through faith in Jesus. In verse 15 we are to be always ready to tell people this gospel message. The only weapon we have is the Spirit's own sword, which is the word of God, the Bible – verse 17. Furthermore, the one thing we must be doing all the time in every possible way is, verse 18, praying, with all kinds of prayers and requests.

Furthermore, it is not enough for just one or two believers to be doing this disconnected from our local Church family. Paul has constantly told us about the love and unity needed in the Church. Our first concern must be to love and encourage one another as we put on the armour together, as a Church fellowship. To put on the armour of God as a Church is to trust in Jesus, study the Bible, pray and share the reality of Jesus with others in the way we live and love.

The armour of God is the gospel of God. We fall into the devil's schemes when we leave this gospel behind. When we don't read the Bible and pray every day we slide into the devil's schemes. It won't be long before we stop living as Jesus commanded and we will no longer tell others about Him.

To put on the armour of God is not some deeper spiritual activity or new discipline that we need to discover. It is standing firm in the simple Way of Jesus– keeping our eyes on the hope of salvation when Jesus returns; answering the accusations of the devil with the righteousness of Christ; exposing the devil's lie with the truth in Jesus.

Each side has just one weapon. The devil – verse 16 – has flaming arrows which are extinguished by trusting Jesus. *Doubt* is the devil's weapon: 'Perhaps *this* life is all you have... and if you keep postponing everything to the new creation you will simply miss out on all the good things... anyway, even if there is a new creation to come, all the most *exciting* things are right now... pie in the sky when you die is just not enough... why suffer now, why be insulted now, why miss out on the good things now, when with a little compromise life can be good... did Jesus *really* say what you think He said?'

The one weapon we have is – verse 17 – the Bible, the spoken words of God. So, the devil says 'did God really say?' and we reply '*Thus* saith the LORD'. This very pattern is exemplified in Jesus own one-to-one with the devil in the wilderness. Remember what John says in 1 John 2:14 – "I write to you, young men, because you are strong, and the word of God lives in you, and you have overcome the evil one."

It is as we live the Way of Jesus that the devil is resisted.

4. Love Jesus with undying love – 6:21-24

Notice how Paul concludes his description of spiritual warfare – verses 19-20. He sees himself engaged in spiritual warfare with the devil. Paul asks for prayer: prayer that he would be constantly engaged in evangelism, in sharing the Way of Jesus. Twice he asks that he would '*fearlessly*' declare the gospel. Obviously Paul felt a lot of fear about telling others about Jesus. He tells us so in 1 Corinthians 2:3. We must never think that Paul was naturally fearless in telling his neighbours about Jesus.

Speaking about Jesus had put him in prison and had made him many enemies. Speaking about Jesus had got him beaten up, filled him with tears and kept him up at night. The devil must have told the great apostle every day that it just wasn't worth it: "*others* would tell these people about Jesus; it wasn't the right time to bring the subject up; it would be more strategic to gain their respect first; don't get stretched too thin; you can't *afford* another sleepless night; you've spoken out so many times before, *this* time doesn't matter; you need to pray about it first; what about your tent-making career..."

Paul's mind must have been full of reasons not to declare the truth about Jesus, so he asked for prayer to speak fearlessly whenever he opened his mouth. It is such a simple prayer request, but it takes us to the very front-line of the conflict showing us where the fighting is heaviest. It is always easier to do what we want rather than follow Jesus. It is always easier to satisfy the cravings of our sinful nature rather than lay down our lives for Jesus and for others.

Perhaps this is why Paul sent Tychicus to the Ephesians – verses 21 and 22. He wanted them to know how he was and what he was doing. He wanted them to see that although he was chained up in prison, he was still faithful to Jesus, still full of the joy that comes from the Spirit. All this would – verse 22 – encourage them.

The conclusion to the whole letter is striking. This letter has shown us that the centre of the universe is a marriage between Jesus Christ, the Eternal Son of the Father, and His Church. Since before the creation of the world, this marriage was planned and prepared. Jesus has defeated all opposition, laying down His life for His Bride, and giving her a pure and spotless life through His mighty resurrection. Joining this Church in expectation of this glorious married future is what life is all about for the whole universe.

The purpose of our existence is to be caught up in an everlasting romance with Jesus the Beloved Son of the Father.

So, verses 23 and 24, love and faith are given to us from God the Father and the Lord Jesus Christ. The undeserved friendship of the Living God is offered to all who love our Lord Jesus Christ with an undying love.

Loving Jesus with an undying love, an incorruptible love: that cuts to the very heart of everything. Nothing matters more than this.

Jesus deserves a much more consistent and lasting love than we ever give Him. What is *anything* in life and death compared to Him? When I put my own short-term interests ahead of Him, they all appear utterly trivial in His presence; after a few minutes in the new creation on resurrection morning, how I will regret that my love for him was so ungenerous, so tight-fisted, so feeble!

Now is the time for us to take these matters to heart, *now* while we still have time to live fruitful Christian lives. The Father created everything because of His great love for Jesus. Let's all learn from the Father and love Jesus too, with an undying love that the devil cannot shake with all his temptations to self-interest and short-term goals.

Study 6 Bible Questions

Ephesians 6:10-20

1. Verse 10 – Is this verse a summary of everything that Paul has been saying in the letter? Could we say that being strong in the LORD and relying on His mighty power have been key themes in the letter? Where have we seen the themes of being 'in Christ' and His mighty 'power' earlier in the letter?
2. Verse 11 – Paul describes us as standing our ground. Why doesn't he describe us as charging into battle?
3. Verse 12 – The unbelief and confusion of the people we witness to and serve is ultimately caused by 'spiritual forces of evil in the heavenly realms'. How does this fact change the way we witness and serve?
4. Verse 13 – Once again Paul insists that we stand our ground. What might 'the day of evil' be? Why do we need God's own armour for such a day?
5. Verse 14 – In order to stand we need truth and righteousness. How has Paul set these before us in this letter to the Ephesians?
6. Verse 15 – Why do we need to be ready with the 'good news of peace'? How does this help us to stand?
7. Verse 16 – If the 'shield of faith' is the answer to the flaming arrows of the evil one, then what does that tell us about the attacks of the evil one? Can we think of how the evil one used this strategy in other parts of the Bible? Have we experienced this in our own lives?
8. Verse 17 – If it is most important to protect our head, then what do we learn about this helmet? The only weapon we have belongs to the Spirit. What does this tell us about the way we use the Word of God?
9. Verse 18 – All around the world the churches that are making an effective stand for Christ are the ones that pray the most. If we think we have enough armour and strength of our own then we do not pray. Why does Paul tell us to pray with "all kinds of prayers and requests"? Why do we need to be 'alert' when we pray for other Christians?
10. Verses 19-20 – How does this prayer request from Paul tell us how the spiritual battles are to be waged? Have we told anyone about the way of Jesus in the past week? What held us back from doing

it? Pray about this right now and, if we are studying together in a group, perhaps we could encourage one another in our witness next time we meet.

Study 6 Further Questions

1. The Bible presents a husband as a servant-head of his wife, but when the model of Christ is lost the self-sacrifice is lost too and then the submission of a wife is much more difficult. The surrounding world – and sometimes even Christians – have become nervous of the language that Paul uses in Ephesians 5:21-33. However, the 'escape' from that Biblical vision has left us with a world with broken marriages, a massive sex industry and the selfish 'pornification' of the culture in general. How can we best present Christ's alternative? How can we avoid being misunderstood?
2. How does a Christian vision of 'parenting' differ from the world's vision? How is Christ Himself to be the centre of the way we bring up our children? How does the presence of Jesus change the way we discipline our children? What is the goal of bringing our children up?
3. How does Jesus influence the way we do our work? How often, if ever, do we mention Him in our workplace or with our colleagues after work? How does Jesus affect 'the Monday morning feeling'? How does He change our career goals? How do we 'fight for our rights' at work if we are following the example of Jesus? Can we fight for the rights of other people?

Study 6 Daily Readings

Day 1	Ephesians 5:21-33
Day 2	Ephesians 6:1-9
Day 3	Ephesians 6:10-24
Day 4	Genesis 2:19-25
Day 5	Deuteronomy 6:1-9
Day 6	Deuteronomy 6:10-25
Day 7	Revelation 19:11-21

The daily Bible readings are an opportunity not only to read through all of the material in the book under study, but also to read parts of the Bible that relate to the themes and issues that we have been considering. Wetry to make sure that we receive light from the whole Bible as we think through the key issues each week.

Suggested Answers to the Bible Study Questions

The New Man

Study 1 Bible Answers

Ephesians 1:15-23

1. Verses 15-16. What two things about the Ephesians cause such thanksgiving in Paul's prayers? Is there any connection between these two things?

The fact that they *trust* Jesus and their *love* for all the Christians. The reason they have love is because they trust Jesus. He shares His love with them and they also obey His commands which show them how to love. The fruit of genuine faith in Christ is always a love for the local Church family.

2. Verse 17. Although the whole Trinity is in this verse, what does Paul pray that the Spirit will do? How might this happen?

He prays that the Holy Spirit would give the Ephesian Church wisdom and revelation so that they would know the Father better. Wisdom is knowing how to live like Christ; knowing what to do and say in all the circumstances of life. Revelation is more to do with seeing and knowing. Throughout this letter we see a strong emphasis on the Church and the gifts of the Spirit working within the Church. So, we would expect the Spirit to bring this wisdom and revelation of the Father as the Church studied and practiced the Scriptures. We will see how the gifts that Christ has given to the Church (Ephesians 4:11-12) are focussed on teaching the Church.

3. Verse 18. Paul prays for more knowledge for the Ephesians, yet this knowledge is not to be grasped by head but heart. Why does this particular knowledge need to be seen with the heart rather than the head?

It is never enough for us to merely know about our heavenly Father. Mere facts are not the wisdom and revelation that the Spirit brings. We are to love and trust our Father, relating to Him in worship and praise. Until our hearts are made alive by the Spirit and then constantly illumined by Him we will not know the Father in the genuine fellowship that we were made for.

4. Verse 19-20. What is the highest example of God's omnipotent power? Why was this a supreme test for the power of the Living God? How is this same power at work in us?

The highest test of the divine power was not the *creation* of the universe but the *redemption* of the universe. On house restoration programmes it is interesting to see how much harder it is to restore an old building than it is to build a new one from scratch. The Almighty power and wisdom of God was needed to make the Eternal, Infinite Word of the Father into a single-celled human being; to live the perfect human life; to die as an atoning sacrifice for the whole cosmos; to bring back an immortal life from death and raise that human life to the highest heaven, filling the entire universe and thereby bringing the whole universe into that new creation future. All this power is at work whenever this great redemption is applied to any sinner who trusts in Jesus and turns from sin.

5. Verse 21. Why do we need to know the extent of Christ's power and authority? What relevance did this have for the Ephesians and what does it mean for us?

The Ephesians lived under the shadow of a mighty pagan empire, in the physical shadow of a vast pagan temple. The message they constantly heard was that Artemis was the great goddess in the spiritual realms. They needed to know that Jesus had ascended to a place of authority far, far above such little 'gods and goddesses'. The same is true for us. It can seem as if the world is ruled by political parties or multinational companies; by religious empires and secular philosophies. Yet, Jesus Christ is still far, far above all these principalities and powers. We can challenge them all in the Name of Jesus, when we understand who He is and His position over all things.

6. Verses 22-23. What do we think of the Church? Does the Bible back up Paul's claim that the Church is at the very centre of the universe, the fullness of Christ Himself who rules everything for the Church? If we believed this, how would we treat our local Church? Do we need to change our priorities?

The Bible always places the Christ and His Church at the very centre of all history. The story of ancient Egypt is just a backdrop for the story of the Church's exodus from slavery in the book of Exodus. The great Babylonian and Persian empires are sideshows to the great story of the Church's exile and restoration. In the book of Daniel we see the empires of the world, in his visions, rising and falling around that one central everlasting kingdom – the stone that became a mountain (see Daniel 2:44-47; Daniel 7:16-18, 26-27).

Study 2 Bible Answers

Ephesians 2:1-10

1. Verse 1 – What does Paul mean by the word 'dead'? How can people be 'dead' if they are also walking around, talking, alive and well?

Jesus Himself described people as 'dead' until they hear His voice and come to life – John 5:24-25. When we are alienated from the life of God by our sin and unbelief then we are disconnected to Life. Jesus is the Life and Light of the world, so if we are disconnected to Him we have no real life in us. Though we may walk around for a time, yet death will certainly take us and keep us.

2. Verse 2 – Many people want to drop out of society and escape the 'rat race'. Some even manage to live on a farm and provide for themselves. If we do this can we avoid the 'ways of this world' that Paul describes in verse 2?

The 'ways of the world' go much deeper than the mere 'rat race'. We carry the ways of the world in our hearts and minds, so we will take them with us to our isolated farm or island. The patterns of selfishness and pride, unbelief and sin, flow out of our sinful heart and we will express them in whatever community (or isolation) we run away to.

3. Verse 3 – Sometimes the cravings of our sinful nature are very obvious: gluttony; lust; greed. How else do these cravings appear, in more subtle ways? What are the 'thoughts' of the sinful nature? What kind of thinking comes naturally to the sinful nature?

The cravings of the flesh also include the desires for praise or social status; for control or popularity. Even 'religion' can so easily become a lust of the flesh, a craving for a form of 'spirituality' or self-righteousness. The sinful nature gives us a way of thinking that is hostile to the Living God. A child does not need to be taught how to be bad, but needs careful discipline to be well behaved. This is because the thoughts of our nature are selfish and chaotic. We invent systems of philosophy and social order that have no reference to the LORD Jesus who sustains all things.

4. Verse 4 – If God is angry with us (verse 3b), then how can He also have 'great love' for us? What does this tell us about the Living

God? Have we ever had an experience where love and anger for somebody all came together at once?

In our own lives, our anger quickly gets out of control, breeding bitterness and hatred. Our anger almost always is sinful and selfish. However, the Father, Son and Holy Spirit are angry with us for our sin, yet that anger is also ruled and controlled in righteousness and holiness. In a similar way, our love can so easily become indulgent and weak, failing to face up to the real issues of goodness, truth and justice. In our sinfulness, our love can excuse evil and descend into mere words and sentiment. However, the love of the Living God never forgets the anger that our sin provokes, yet will go to such extraordinary lengths to deal with our sin so that we can escape the consequences of what we have done.

5. Verse 5 – How does the second part of verse 5 connect to the first part? Why does Paul conclude the verse with "it is by grace you have been saved"? How does the first part of the verse lead to that conclusion?

We were dead in our disobedience. We were unable to establish a bridge to the Living God. In fact, in our sinful isolation from Christ, we did not even want to find Him and were overwhelmed by pagan superstition, hedonistic slavery and lost ignorance. Yet, Christ died for us and rose again into a righteous and immortal human life even when the human race was utterly lost in sin and godlessness. We have no way to make ourselves alive, yet even in deepest and darkest mess the LORD Jesus can raise us up into newness of life. This proves that our salvation is always due only to the undeserved free friendship of the Living God and can never be a human achievement in the slightest degree.

6. Verse 6 – Why was it so important for the Ephesians to know that they had been raised up to the highest heaven with Jesus? How does this verse have the same impact for us today? What are the claims and assumptions, the philosophies and myths that would threaten us in the world of today?

17 Will Durant, Caesar and Christ (New York: Simon and Schuster, 1944), p. 652

The Ephesians lived under the shadow of a mighty pagan empire, in the physical shadow of a vast pagan temple. The message they constantly heard was that Artemis was the great goddess in the spiritual realms. They might have felt as if they were insignificant and worthless beneath such principalities and powers. Yet, they needed to know that Jesus places the Church right next to Him in the highest heaven. We do not need to serve or submit to these pagan and political powers, no matter how impressive they may seem.

7. Verse 7 – How have the great riches of God's grace been shown through the Ephesian Church down through the ages? How can the life of our own local churches display these riches? Where is the kindness of God in Christ Jesus most clearly displayed?

Today the cult of Artemis of the Ephesians is long gone. Nobody today would ever worship that ancient and worthless goddess. Her great temple has long been reduced to rubble. Yet, the Church at Ephesus outlived the cult of Artemis and we are the distant children of what happened in the Name of Jesus in first century Ephesus. We can today marvel at the power and glory of Jesus in maintaining His Church against all her enemies. Historian Will Durant observed, "Caesar and Christ had met in the arena and Christ had won".[17]

8. Verse 8-9 – Why does Paul say that even coming to trust Jesus is a gift that God gives to us? We can see that saving ourselves is too much for us, but surely can't we trust and love Jesus no matter how messed up we are?

Our problem goes deeper than we ever realise. Our sinful 'death' does not just stay at a superficial level but goes right down into who we are and the workings of our heart. Our corruption has ruined the desires of our heart so that we do not desire or trust the LORD Jesus until the Holy Spirit Himself works within us. Until the Spirit shows us the wonder and truth of Jesus our hearts are captured by other 'loves' that blind us, even the self-centred love of ourselves.

9. Verse 10 – Is there anything at all for us to do? If even faith is given to us, then shouldn't we do as little as possible to make sure that none of our works get in the way? Is it wrong to even speak about 'obeying the commands of God', because that might drive us into a 'works' way of thinking?

Faith and not works is the central issue. We are never able to attract or earn or attain the friendship of the Living God. When we simply trust Jesus alone then He makes us alive even when we were dead; He forgives our sin; He lifts us up to the highest heaven. However, as we trust Jesus then we trust His commands also. We trust that when He tells us what to do not only is it the right thing to do but that He will also enable us to do it. The man with the withered hand was commanded to stretch out his hand, which was impossible for him to do. Yet, because the man trusted Jesus he still obeyed and found that the command of Jesus was more amazing than he imagined! Trusting Jesus always involves obeying Jesus, not out of a need to prove or earn His love or forgiveness, but always simply as an expression of our trust and love for Him. He sets us free from the ways of life that ruined us and brings us into that wide open space of His Way.

Study 3 Bible Answers

Ephesians 3:1-13

1. Verse 1 – Why does Paul describe himself as a 'prisoner' of Jesus Christ? What does this tell us about his life and mission?

In chapter 4:1 he describes himself as a prisoner for the sake of Jesus, but first he here describes himself as a prisoner of Jesus. He is acknowledging that he does not belong to himself, that he cannot follow his own desires or will. Jesus Himself said that He always does the will of His Father; that He did not want to do His own will (Luke 22:42). So Paul follows in the way of Jesus and makes it clear that whether he is in a Roman prison or not, yet he is always and everywhere the prisoner of Jesus. Paul's whole life is freedom from sin, but slavery to Jesus Christ (see Romans 6:15-23)

2. Verses 2-3 – Paul assumes they have already heard his testimony about how Jesus confronted him and sent him off to the non-Jewish world. Why does he want to remind them of this and the fact that the 'mystery' or 'secret' was made known to him by personal revelation?

Paul's testimony is an important part of his authority as an apostle. Paul did not appoint himself to be an apostle and did not give himself this task of carrying the message of Jesus into such dangerous new territories. Paul was addressed and commanded by Jesus Himself. He was sent by his Master to do His will and the message he was given was not his own but given by the personal instruction of Jesus Himself. When Paul told the other apostles what Jesus had told him the other apostles agreed that it was the true message of Jesus (see Galatians 2:9).

3. Verses 4-6 – Three times in these verses Paul speaks of a 'mystery'. In English a 'mystery' is something that we can't understand, but in Greek it is a 'secret' that has become known. However, Paul just tells us in simple language what this 'secret' is in verse 6. How does this 'secret' explain some of the biggest confrontations in the life of Paul? Does this 'secret' help us to understand the book of Acts?

The secret is that the Gentiles and the Jews are joined together as one body in Jesus. In the past the Gentiles had to become Jewish in order to

join the Church but now the Church was to be administered in a different way so that Gentiles could remain as uncircumcised Gentiles and yet be members of the Church/Israel. In the book of Acts and in the New Testament letters we see this issue come up time after time as the Church got hold of this new administration of the Church. Some people found it hard to let go of the way that the Law had administered the Church and wanted to insist on circumcision for Church membership. Others even believed that it was the Law that had saved people, and these were the false teachers that caused so much trouble in the book of Acts.

4. Verses 4-6 – If Paul's life has been shaped by this 'secret', how does verse 1 connect to verse 5?

Paul's own mission directly relates to that. Jesus perswonally appointed him to be one of the key pioneers in sharing this ancient secret with the whole world. Paul did not appoint himself to this work, but went out at Christ's command to explain from the ancient Scriptures how it had always been God's intention to bring the Gentiles in to the Church family. He is a prisoner of the LORD Jesus and his life was dedicated to serving the advance of the Church from Israel to all the Gentiles.

5. Whenever Paul writes about the salvation of the Gentiles, he keeps going back to the ancient Hebrew Scriptures: to Moses, the Prophets and the Psalms – see for example, Romans 9:24-29 and Romans 15:7-12. So, what does Paul mean by verse 5?

It was always very clear that Christ was saving both Jews and Gentiles. There are countless examples of that throughout the Hebrew Scriptures. However, when Gentiles were saved they had to leave behind their Gentile nationality and become Israelites, circumcised members of the ancient Church. The Edomites and Philistines, the Egyptians and Moabites could no longer be members of those nations but joined the tribes of Israel – see Exodus 12:38; Deuteronomy 29:10-15; Joshua 6:25; 9:26-27; Ruth 1:16; 4:13-22; Esther 8:17; Isaiah 56:3-7. However, the fact that Jesus Christ would abolish the temporary system of Law by His death and resurrection so that the Gentiles could remain as members of the Gentile nations was only made clear to the Church in the time of the apostles. Jesus sent His disciples out to the whole world, beginning at Jerusalem, Judea, Samaria and then onto all the other nations. The very fact that at the Feast of Pentecost in Acts the believers were given the ability to speak all the languages of the world was a sign of this global nature of Israel.

6. Verses 7-8 – How would we describe Paul's charismatic gift from God?

Paul may have had all kinds of charismatic gifts including the ability to speak many Gentile languages (see 1 Corinthians 14:18), yet all his individual gifts were part of his overall gift of reaching the Gentiles. Paul himself said that it was his mission to take the news of Jesus to people who had not yet been reached – Romans 15:20.

7. Verse 9 – If the secret is "Jews and Gentiles joined together as one body in Jesus Christ", then why was the administration of this kept hidden for such long ages? Why does Paul remind us that God created all things?

The LORD God created all humanity from Adam. The different nations of the world are all part of the same human family, all equally created by the Living God. His purpose has always been to save the whole human family, reaching people of every tribe and nation, language and culture. While the world waited for the birth of the Promised Messiah, the world had to come to that one nation of Israel to find life and truth – see 1 Kings 10:24 for a powerful example of this happening. The Law given through Moses formed a wall around the ancient Church, separating the Church away from the Gentile nations. When Christ accomplished all that was prophesied of Him and He abolished the dividing wall of the Law (see Ephesians 2:14-16). Now it was time for the Church to spread out across the whole world, just as Christ Himself ascended to fill the whole universe.

8. Verse 10-11 – Why must the unified Body of Christ be displayed to the whole world, in every nation? Why is it so important that the united, loving Body of Jesus be displayed so clearly?

The eternal purpose of the Father was to display His own power and wisdom specifically through the Church of Jesus Christ. It is through the Church that we see the reality of the Living God. It is through the Church that the revelation of God is explained and displayed. It is through the

Church that the world may come to know, serve and worship this Living God. In addition, all the principalities and powers in the heavenly realms watch as the Church of the Living God displays His power and wisdom. It is very important that we live carefully and obediently because our local Church is the Living God on display to our local area.

9. Verses 12-13 – What was the value of Paul's sufferings? Why did he keep on serving and speaking even when it got him in so much trouble? What will we do that would bring the same glory, even if it also brings the same sufferings?

Paul was prepared to go through all his hard work, sleepless nights and persecution because the fruit of it was Gentile people joining in the ancient Church of the Living God. Gentiles who had been without God and without hope were now, through trusting Jesus, approaching "God with freedom and confidence" (verse 12). So, although it may have seemed very discouraging for Paul and his supporters to face so much suffering, if they could see it all from the perspective of God's eternal purpose, then the true glory of the situation could be seen.

Study 4 Bible Answers

Ephesians 4:1-13

1. Verse 1 – If we look back at the end of chapter 3, what is the high calling that should shape the way we live?

Our high calling is nothing less than to imitate the Living God. We are to be filled with the fullness of God as we are caught up into the infinite love and knowledge of Christ. This calling must fill our hearts and minds, pushing all other hopes and dreams into their proper place. If this incredible hope lies before us then we must strain towards it, living it out as much as possible even now.

2. Verse 2 – When the Father can do immeasurably more than we can ask or imagine, how can the instructions of verse 2 live up to such great power? Is this really the most that Paul can imagine?

When we remember what our situation was in 2:1-3 and if we also know our own hearts, then it is indeed almost unimaginable for people like us to be 'completely humble and gentle'. Pride and selfishness are so deeply woven into our old self that it really does require the full extent of divine power for us to live the loving and patient life of Christ.

3. Verse 3 – Why does Paul say 'make every effort' to keep united in the Spirit? How much effort do we normally put into this? Are there ever times when all our efforts are not enough to keep the unity of the Spirit?

We must do all we can to keep unity and peace. There are times when no matter what we do yet there are others who are determined to bring division. The situation is not always completely under our control. In Romans 12:18 we read "if it is possible, as far as it depends on you, live at peace with everyone." The question is, how much effort do we really put into this? We must never allow the sun to set on our arguments and anger. We need to speak to people to make peace, even if it was not our fault, just as Christ did so much to make peace when He is blameless.

4. Verses 4-6 – Consider all the items that Paul lists that are 'one'. Can we think of one consequence of each that should hold us all together? For example, if we all have the same baptism then we are all joined together as members of the same community, separated from the world.

One Body – we work together and build each other up. We cannot live without each other.

One Spirit – The same Holy Spirit who equips me and gives me experience of Christ and illumines the Scriptures is also in all the other members of the Body.

One hope – We will spend all eternity together in the new creation, filled with the fullness of God. We have to get on with each other because we are joined together for eternal ages.

One Lord – We are all servants of the same Divine Master, the LORD Jesus. His commands and example are given to each of us. We must all conform to the same pattern of life.

One faith – Although we might differ about many things in life and have different tastes and opinions, yet at the centre of our lives we trust in Jesus. We believe the same gospel message and this must be the most important truth we hold, setting everything else to the side.

One God and Father – Over all the world, over all creation, over all the Church family is our heavenly Father who bothers to number every hair on the heads of each one of us. We are all in the great family of the Father, under His love and provision.

5. Verse 7 – The friendship of Jesus has been given to each one of us – but this friendship gives us abilities and responsibilities. Why does Paul insist that this empowering friendship of Jesus is given to "each one of us"?

Every member of the Church family is important and each one of us has an important part to play. The Holy Spirit applies the treasures that Jesus gives to each member of our fellowship and we need all the gifts He has given. None of us can be ignored. If our Church family does not give opportunities for us all to serve together then we need to think again about how we live and work together.

6. Verse 8 – The Hebrew of Psalm 68:18 perhaps should be translated as "He received gifts for men", but Paul brings out the relevant meaning here by quoting it as "gave gifts to men". How does Psalm 68:17-20 fill out our understanding of the ascension of Jesus?

Psalm 68:17 – the huge heavenly armies are all at the disposal of the LORD God who ascends back to heaven from His victory. We can have great confidence in the power of heaven that stands behind us in every situation. Read 2 Kings 6:8-23 for a wonderful example of this – "those who are with us are more than those who are with them"

Psalm 68:18 – The whole world is taken 'captive' by the victorious LORD Jesus. He is the LORD God who ascends to His home in heaven, with even His enemies forced to acknowledge His rule.

Psalm 68:19 – This LORD God who ascends to the highest heaven with all power, not only fills the universe with His glorious resurrected presence, but He "daily bears our burdens". He is the Great High Priest who represents us: He is the God-Man who is the fullness of God and also the fullness of humanity all at once.

Psalm 68:20 – This Sovereign LORD and Saving God specifically saves us from death. Death might seem to be the great and final enemy that nobody can delay or defeat, yet this ascended LORD Jesus is fully able to give us 'escape from death'. The reason that He has ascended on high is that He first defeated death.

7. Verse 9 – Psalm 68 verse 18 and verse 24 can sound strange at first. Why is the LORD God ascending? Why does he need to go back into heaven? How do Paul's comments in Ephesians 4:9 help us understand what is happening in Psalm 68?

Paul explains that the very fact that we read of God 'ascending' means that He must have first of all descended down to earth to accomplish His great victory. In popular 'folk religion' there is an idea that 'god' is in heaven all the time or that he is nowhere and everywhere all at once. However, when we are confronted by the Living God of the Bible all our assumptions and human ideas fall down. Here is an Almighty God who created the heavens and the earth; an infinite God who cannot be contained by the entire universe; yet, He impossibly comes down from the highest heaven to live a human life, die our death, rise from death and then return to the highest heaven in triumph in order to fill the entire universe with His glorious presence.

8. Verse 10 – When we read the gospels we are sometimes shown how Jesus was tired, hungry, thirsty or sad, yet there are other times we see Him walking on water, commanding the weather, talking to Moses and Elijah who had been dead for hundreds of years, raising the dead and forgiving sins. When He was walking on earth, Jesus was also sustaining the entire universe. Why is it so important to remember that the same Man who was crucified now fills the whole universe? How does this connect to the vast vision of the love and knowledge of Jesus at the end of chapter 3?

Jesus is the Great High Priest over all creation. The Eternal Word of the Father is a human being, a citizen of planet earth! Yes, there are depths and wonders here that go beyond all our systems and all our imagination, but the whole realm of nature is ruled and sustained by this Great High Priest. As we grow up into the love and knowledge of Jesus we are taken up into such expansive and vast realms of thought and experience, far beyond all that we have ever known. When we read the gospel stories we are actually reading the life of the Person who is the life and logic of the entire universe.

Two wonderful quotations from C. H. Spurgeon – "Immanuel, God with us in our nature, in our sorrow, in our lifework, in our punishment, in our grave, and now with us, or rather we with Him, in resurrection, ascension, triumph, and Second Advent, splendour."

"Infinite, and an infant. Eternal, and yet born of a woman. Almighty, and yet hanging on a woman's breast. Supporting a universe, and yet needing to be carried in a mother's arms. King of angels, and yet the reputed son of Joseph. Heir of all things, and yet the carpenter's despised son."

9. Verse 11 – Why does Jesus use the vast resources of the entire universe to provide leadership and good teaching in the local churches? Aren't there more important ways to use such cosmic power?

If the great goal is that everything in heaven and earth be brought together under Christ for the Church, who is His fullness (Ephesians 1:23), then the Church is at the very centre of the universe. Everything else in history and around the universe, whether the birth of stars or the fall of empires, is a mere sideshow compared to the growth into maturity of the local Churches.

10. Verse 12 – What is the main responsibility of the preachers, evangelists, pastors and teachers? How much time should an evangelist spend with not-yet-Christians and how much time training the Christians?

Their main job is to train and equip the whole Church family for living out the life and way of Jesus. They must not try to do all the work on their own because this would deny the Church family their part in the work. So, an evangelist who goes off on his own to do evangelism is not doing his job properly. He needs to put effort into training and inspiring the Church family in their own evangelism.

11. Verse 13 – Given the truly incredible and breath-taking view of Jesus that Paul sets before us here, how does this motivate us to push onto maturity, unity and knowledge of Jesus?

We are part of something that is so big: stretching back into eternity past and on into the eternal future. We are members of a local Church, which is the most important thing happening in our local area. The universe itself finds its fulfilment as the Church grows into the fullness of Jesus Christ. Jesus Himself uses all the resources of heaven and earth in order to equip us for the work of witness and service. We cannot afford to waste our time fighting with each other or grieving the Spirit.

Walk in love, light and wisdom

Study 5 Bible Answers

Ephesians 4:29-5:7

1. Verse 29 – If we are to avoid 'rotten' speech, what are the three essential features that Paul sets out for all of our speech?

i. Words that are *helpful for building others up*; words that are kind and well intentioned.

ii. Words that are *necessary*; words that deal with genuine needs.

iii. Words that are of *benefit* to those who listen. It is important that the words are spoken and heard in the right way.

2. Verse 30 – Why does Paul suddenly warn us about grieving the Holy Spirit in the middle of these commands? What does this tell us about what grieves the Spirit?

The way we speak and treat each other is at the very heart of the Holy Spirit's work. When we say 'the grace' together we pray for the 'fellowship of the Holy Spirit' to be with us. The mark of spiritual life and maturity is the love that we show one another in practical actions and loving speech. The Spirit is always most grieved when we damage the fellowship that He brings.

3. Verse 31-32 – How does the example of God in Christ (verse 32) stand as the opposite of all the things listed in verse 31?

We have done so much wrong against the Living God, as a race and in our own individual lives. However, instead of becoming bitter about this and allowing His anger or rage to respond with immediate vengeance, the Father, Son and Holy Spirit acted out of love and patience, going to infinite lengths to reconcile us to Himself. Instead of fighting against us, he pleads with us to accept peace with Him while there is still time. He has no malice or slander against us but always tell us the truth and offers us nothing but good.

4. Chapter 5, verse 1-2 – Satan originally tempted us to be like God, but his way of doing that led to the murder of the whole human race. What is the true way to imitate the Living God? Why does Paul tell us to be like God "as dearly loved children"?

In Genesis 3, in alliance with the devil, we tried to be like God in deciding for ourselves what was right and wrong. Instead we are to be like God in trusting His judgment of right and wrong, and therefore imitating His way of life. We live as He lives; we are holy as He is holy; we are perfect as He is perfect, loving our enemies and serving others before ourselves. Just as love has eternally been the central feature of the life of God, so we pursue this love in our own Church fellowships. We can live this life because we are "dearly loved children": we have been born again into the family of God, given His very nature in that 'new self' that we can now put on (Ephesians 4:24).

5. Verse 3 – Why is Paul so very careful about even a 'hint' of sexual immorality? Why is this such a powerful desire, in the light of verses 1-2?

If the centre of the life of the Living God is love, and therefore we are created to live out such love and fellowship, then our sexuality is obviously one of the most powerful aspects of human life. We cannot afford to play around with this in any way. Even the slightest hint of immorality can cause terrible consequences. We are not strong enough to control this area of life without the Father, Son and Holy Spirit.

6. Verse 4 – What kind of good speech is the cure for all the bad speech? Why is that? What kind of attitude does each produce?

Thanksgiving is the cure for our bad speech. When our words and prayers are full of gratitude then we look at the whole of life very differently. Instead of viewing things with a cynical or selfish eye we see things in terms of grace and goodness. When we take time each day to thank our heavenly Father for all His care and provision we are rejecting the old self and its selfish approach to life.

7. Verse 5 – How can anybody be saved if this verse is true? These sins are found in all of us, so can any of us ever enter the kingdom of Christ?

This reminds us of the issue of 'unintentional sins' in Leviticus 4 and 5 and Numbers 15. Do we love our sins or do we hate them? Do we wish that we never did them, that they could be cut out from us at any cost, or does our regret quickly turn to new plans for the same sins? What is at

the centre of our life or what defines us? If our life is defined by trusting and following Jesus and we long to be forever free of our sin, then we are in the kingdom of Christ. However, if these sins define who we are and what we think about or desire then until we repent there can be no place for us in His kingdom. If we truly confess our sins and turn from them to Christ then He will cleanse us from all our sin.

8. Verses 6-7 – There are always people who say that God will not really judge the world, that in the end He will overlook all these sins. How should we deal with such people? Does it make a difference whether these people claim to be Christians or not?

Throughout the whole Bible one of the most dangerous lies of all is to play down or even reject the warnings of God's Word. The mark of the false prophet was always to reassure people or even proclaim 'peace, peace' even as the judgment of God was approaching (Jeremiah 6:14). The problem is that such false prophets *seem* to be more 'loving' at a superficial level. If these people claim to be Christians we need to stay as far away from them as possible and if they are trying to get into our local Church we need to exclude them. We must make it clear to the watching world that they do not speak for us or for the Bible.

9. If our goal as a local Church is to live the life of the Living God, then what practical changes can we make in the coming weeks to guide us nearer to that?

The mystery of union in Christ

Study 6 Bible Answers

Ephesians 6:10-20

1. Verse 10 – Is this verse a summary of everything that Paul has been saying in the letter? Could we say that being strong in the LORD and relying on His mighty power have been key themes in the letter? Where have we seen the themes of being 'in Christ' and His mighty 'power' earlier in the letter?

The whole of the first chapter was focussed on the fact that the Church is "in Christ". All the blessings that the Father has for us are stored up in Christ. The whole universe is purposed for the Church in Christ! The mighty power of the Living God is used for the salvation and exaltation of the Church – see Ephesians 2:4-7; 3:20-21. The power of God in Christ is what enables us to actually live as God lives, even though we live in a world that is filled with the lies and schemes of the devil.

2. Verse 11 – Paul describes us as standing our ground. Why doesn't he describe us as charging into battle?

The whole creation belongs to Christ and His Church. Christ rules over the whole creation, filling it all with His resurrected and glorified presence. We are standing our ground in our home, our future inheritance. The devil and his spiritual forces want to invade this world and destroy us. We are ultimately standing on our home ground, whereas the devil has no ground to call his own. He will finally be thrown out of the creation into the outer darkness, together with all that belong to him. There is no final place here for the forces of evil. We stand our ground trusting that the armies of heaven will finally clear the field of all invaders.

3. Verse 12 – The unbelief and confusion of the people we witness to and serve is ultimately caused by 'spiritual forces of evil in the heavenly realms'. How does this fact change the way we witness and serve?

We can keep our attention fixed on sharing the Way, the Truth and the Life of Jesus without becoming caught up in individual conflict. We are every aware that unless the Holy Spirit opens the eyes of an unbelieving person they will never, by their own efforts or desire, trust in Jesus. Our desire is not to win arguments but to win souls for Christ (Proverbs 11:20).

4. Verse 13 – Once again Paul insists that we stand our ground. What might 'the day of evil' be? Why do we need God's own armour for such a day?

When we consider what happening in Acts 19 then 'the day of evil' probably would mean times of severe persecution, perhaps when members of the Church are arrested or their lives threatened. When the opposition of the evil one comes out in naked violence and oppression, it is very easy for our witness and stand to collapse. On that day will we still speak up and stand up for Jesus? That 'day of evil' can also be the times of hardship and suffering in our lives when we also might allow the circumstances to shake our foundations.

5. Verse 14 – In order to stand we need truth and righteousness. How has Paul set these before us in this letter to the Ephesians?

It may be possible that Paul is referring to the righteous status that is given to us when we trust Jesus, but if we look back at how he has spoken of righteousness in this letter it is more likely that Paul is thinking about the righteous behaviour that flows from that new humanity of Jesus. So, in Ephesians 4:22-24 we must put off the old self and put on the new self created to be like God in true righteousness. This is the truth that we need to know when the world around us tells us that we have no option but to sin. In Ephesians 5:9 the themes of righteousness and truth come together when we learn that the fruit of the light I righteousness and truth.

6. Verse 15 – Why do we need to be ready with the 'good news of peace'? How does this help us to stand?

It is all too easy to turn our attention inwards on our own problems, especially when we are under pressure from the world, the flesh and the devil. It is vital that we are always ready to share the good news with others, even with those who are opposing us. This is the gospel that brings peace and the only thing that can change the hearts and minds of those that oppose us.

7. Verse 16 – If the 'shield of faith' is the answer to the flaming arrows of the evil one, then what does that tell us about the attacks of the evil one? Can we think of how the evil one used this strategy in other parts of the Bible? Have we experienced this in our own lives?

The devil's great weapon is doubt. He loves to undermine and question the truth in Jesus. If he can make us doubt the truth then the way we live will quickly collapse. With Eve in Genesis 3 he asked 'did God really say...?' With Jesus he asked Jesus to prove who He is rather than simply trusting His Father. Satan will cast doubt on the doctrines but also the practice of the Bible. If we will hold the doctrines without ever putting it into practice then he has caused us to doubt in the deepest way.

8. Verse 17 – If it is most important to protect our head, then what do we learn about this helmet? The only weapon we have belongs to the Spirit. What does this tell us about the way we use the Word of God?

Salvation is the central purpose of the gospel – 1 Peter 1:9. The Ephesian letter has shown us our desperate state under the power of the devil in 2:1-3. We cannot possibly stand unless we have been given this salvation in Jesus but also we need to know this salvation for ourselves. We need that assurance of our salvation that comes from trusting Jesus, bearing His fruit and experiencing His presence with us – all of which Paul has described in the letter.

9. Verse 18 – All around the world the churches that are making an effective stand for Christ are the ones that pray the most. If we think we have enough armour and strength of our own then we do not pray. Why does Paul tell us to pray with "all kinds of prayers and requests"? Why do we need to be 'alert' when we pray for other Christians?

Paul does not want our times of prayer restricted to formal prayer meetings once a week. We need to be praying in all kinds of ways throughout each and every day. We can quickly give thanks for any of the good things that we receive from the Father each day or ask for wisdom throughout the day or pray for each person we meet or commit our various activities in prayer many times in the day or pray through all that happened as we go to bed. Quick prayers of one sentence and longer prayers of meditation and fellowship are all part of our life of prayer. Whether we use prepared forms of words or spontaneous outpourings of the heart, we need to turn to prayer over and over again in lots of different forms and ways and occasions.

10. Verses 19-20 – How does this prayer request from Paul tell us how the spiritual battles are to be waged? Have we told anyone about the way of Jesus in the past week? What held us back from doing it? Pray about this right now and, if we are studying together in a group, perhaps we could encourage one another in our witness next time we meet.

If the world is in as desperate state as Ephesians 2:1-3 describes, then it is vital that we live and speak as clear, courageous witnesses of Jesus. The devil wants us to doubt the Bible and doubt the Way of Jesus. Whether through fear or apathy, he will try to silence us in any way he can. Paul knew that the test of whether he was standing firm in the power of God was whether he was speaking of Jesus as the opportunities arose. Recently a godly Christian mentioned that every time he had genuinely asked God to give him an opportunity to talk about Jesus, the Father had always presented one. Yes, let's get more training from evangelists in how to do this well (as Ephesians 4:11-13 tells us), but let's start with what we can do right now.